Sharing Digital Photos
The Future of Memories

dane m. howard

Group By: Keyword

Tell a story...
Edit Picture...
Send in E-mail...
Print...

Find Similar Picture
Go to Picture Location

Convert File Format...
Edit Keywords...

Cut
Copy
Delete
Rename
Properties...

www.futureofmemories.com

PUBLISHED BY
Microsoft Press
A Division of Microsoft Corporation
One Microsoft Way
Redmond, Washington 98052-6399

Library of Congress Cataloging-in-Publication Data

Howard, Dane M., 1971–
  Sharing Digital Photos: The Future of Memories
        p. cm.
     Includes index.
     ISBN 0-7356-1992-1
     1. Photographs—Conservation and restoration—Data processing. 2. Photography—Digital techniques.
     3. Photograph albums—Data processing. 4. Scrapbooks—Data processing. 5. Digital preservation. I. Title.

  TR465.H69 2003
  775—dc22   2003059362

Printed and bound in the United States of America.

1 2 3 4 5 6 7 8 9   QWT   8 7 6 5 4

Distributed in Canada by H.B. Fenn and Company Ltd.

A CIP catalogue record for this book is available from the British Library.

Microsoft Press books are available through booksellers and distributors worldwide. For further information about international editions, contact your local Microsoft Corporation office or contact Microsoft Press International directly at fax (425) 936-7329. Visit our Web site at www.microsoft.com/learning/books/. Send comments to *mspinput@microsoft.com*.

Acquisitions Editor: David Dwyer
Project Editor: Kristine Haugseth
Indexer: Patricia Masserman

Body Part No. X10-09373

For Chloe, Tucker, and Lori.

Sharing with you is the most fun…
I will ever have.

table of contents

Introduction, 1

SECTION 1
You Have a Story to Tell. Let's Go! 7

SECTION 2
More Effective Images, 55

SECTION 3
Organizing Your Living Library, 117

SECTION 4
Sharing Your Memories, 151

Afterword, 191

Contributors, 195

Appendix, 209

Index, 219

Acknowledgments

I must first thank my wonderful wife, Lori. You enable me. You are a brilliant wife and mother. Memories are better when shared with you.

Chloe and Tucker...Thank you for your spirit and your wonder. Dad loves you.

A book like this is a labor of love. I will have to thank my experienced publishing team for their vision and experience. Don Fowley, thank you for "reserving" the right to do this project and your thoughtful vision to place me in such good hands. Chris Nelson and David Dwyer, thank you for your artful ability to craft and shape this project. Patricia Bradbury, Linda LaFlamme, and Kim Scott, thank you helping me tighten the pieces and produce the bits.

Thanks to my contributors and advisors. You are truly artisans of innovation.

Ammon Haggerty, Asta Glatzer, Chad Nelson, Charles Mauzy, Christian Colando, Chris Nelson, Christian Anthony, Curtis Wong, Damon Nelson, David Dwyer, Don Fowley, Don Barnett, Donald Thompson, Emily Palmgren, Eric Cheng, Eric Rodenbeck, Jae Park, Kristine Haugseth, Jeff Boettcher, Jeff Fong, Jeff Koch, Jonathan Cluts, Josh Ulm, Kentaro Toyama, Kim Scott, Linda LaFlamme, Lili Cheng, Michael Gough, Michael Ninness, Patricia Bradbury, Sean Kelly, and William Lamb.

...and thank you to my parents, who have always been a support in my life.

About the Author

Dane M. Howard has been telling stories with pictures for 12 years. As a designer and director of the creative process, he has developed creative strategies and products for Microsoft, BMW, Major League Baseball, Quokka Sports, NBCOlympics, Rolling Stone, Pulse Entertainment, and Disney. His clients and collaborators include key management of design, marketing, research and development, and chief executives.

As a designer and now as a father, Dane is using his background in sequential media and experience-based design to express his passion for sharing the stories of his loved ones. His search has brought him to discover existing and evolving technologies that will shape the future of digital photography and self-publishing for the mass market. The reinvention and expression of narrative is carefully observed and evident in his work and research.

He maintains a personal project to document the events of his family. The interest in this project (**www.chloehoward.com**) spawned this book to tell others how to document and share life's events. He is also an accomplished oil painter and is fortunate to exhibit his paintings in both New York and California.

Dane is the design manager for Microsoft's Smart Personal Objects Group in Redmond, Washington.

www.futureofmemories.com

Foreword

Memory Sharing

Stories build in strength with the retelling. Oral traditions in storytelling are based on this simple fact. The success of novels, television, and movies is predicated on the same idea—you need to build a community of interest, a growing body of shared knowledge and enthusiasm, if you want the story to thrive.

Today's stories are the providence of mass media. They depend on mass appeal for the economic success that is needed to get them recorded, promoted, and distributed.

Memories are similarly structured—they build in power with sharing. There are powerful memories that are held in private, singular remembrances that might require effort to maintain, but shared memories are a different beast. When they are shared among family or friends or acquaintances, they gain in substance. Every sharing breathes life into the memory, rounds it out, and reaffirms it.

Enter digital technology. The opportunities created by the ability to effortlessly store, present, and distribute memories are creating a revolution. The power of mass media, the ability to build stories that are relevant to mass audiences, is suddenly available to smaller, more discrete audiences—communities of interest the size of a couple or family or affinity group or fan club or—you name it. The simple act of converting memories, maintained in text, photos, audio, or video, to bits, frees those memories from the constraints that apply to mass media. It even frees those memories from the typical boundaries of physical space. The photo on the mantle, the powerful mnemonic device that reminds one of a certain summer day or a first meeting is, in digital form, free to float in and out of the conscience of as many people as it is distributed to—all through the power of digital technologies.

These digital memories can be retrieved at any time, they can be sent to others, and they can be combined and recombined, building in power with every viewing. Digitally enabled, memories are free to find their audience and to grow.

The photographs and video and salutations in the cards at my daughter's thirteenth birthday are not exactly ready for prime time, at least not the prime time that needs millions of viewers to justify its existence. But to a specific audience, her family and friends, there are stories to be told. And these stories become memories of increasing power with every telling. We look at the slide show, and we remember. We can combine the images of a 13-year-old with pictures of her at 6 on the same beach, and the memories build. Grandmother, in Florida, views the same show and throws in recollections of a different beach on a different day. The power of the memory builds.

The bits are flying everywhere. The picture of a close friend's wedding is captured on a cell phone, and immediately available on my laptop while I'm checking my e-mail at the local wireless-enabled coffee shop. I don't just view it. I save it. Then I attach it to a few e-mails to mutual friends. I love the suit, so I throw in a picture of the one I got married in. That memory will live for a long long time.

In only a few short years, the techniques for capture and the range of digital cameras and recorders have exploded. The revolution has increased as rapidly as the cost has gone down. There is also a wide range of services for storing and distributing images. Although this new form of digital memory support is in its infancy, there are already patterns and styles of narrative that clearly illustrate its power. Simple reproduction of the layout of a photo album has been supplanted by elaborate layered and woven presentations that support more complex (and engaging) narratives. Advanced interfaces have replaced conventional paging, supporting wandering and traveling through the content in ways that spark additional memories. Presentation is being replaced by experience—you don't just use a photograph as mnemonic device; you "experience" the memory digitally.

Like every revolution in narrative, the future of digital memories is hard to imagine. One thing is clear, though—the memories will get richer and stronger—and that should be a good thing.

—**Michael Gough**
  Chief Creative Officer, Macromedia
  Father of Two

introduction

The physical album creates a memorial of our vacation, while its online version keeps the memory fresh and alive. Having access to both extends our memory of our trip.

We arrived the next day, but it felt like one long day. We arrived in Zurich and had a lot of stuff. We got a lot of smiles from the locals, who just couldn't believe three people had too much stuff. She shook it off and waited for the train. The luggage carts are way better than the one's here in the states. I watched a lady push one onto the escalator to get down to the train. I followed her lead. The train system was our first taste of a remarkable rail system. It's very well organized and tremendously ef

scroll for more

The Events That Shape Our Lives

My life changed in 2000. I can remember the excitement that hit me surrounding the birth of my daughter, Chloe. The significance of that event was something that changed me as a person and motivated me to do things I wouldn't normally do. I felt compelled to reach out and bring my family and friends closer. With friends and family all over the world, I decided to create an online memory album to keep them in touch.

The fundamental change is where we are keeping and distributing our memories.

I'm still surprised at the body of work that has since filled up Chloe's website over the years (and my hard drive!). I have changed the, "Hey, do you want to see my kid?" routine to, "Did you see what she did this week?" Grandparents, friends, and colleagues have become more immersed in Chloe as a person and feel closer to us as a family. When we gave our daughter her first birthday party, it was amazing how many of our friends referred to the stories and memories that we had shared on her site. They had been invested in her story for an entire year and were now valuable members of our family's community.

everywhere you want. At this point we were all running on vapors, and were eager to find our Hotel. chloe was in good spirits once mommy gave her some snacks. We were **onto Interlaken**. Chloe Index

The Future Should Be About…

You.

What will make you an effective author of your memories?

You might change your camera, your PC, or your hard drive a dozen times, but your memories will be forever.

When I think about the future of memories, I think about having more potential.

> **The potential to tell better stories**

> **The potential to access and distribute memories more effectively**

> **The potential to build and author them faster**

Over the years, I've learned the importance of telling effective and simple stories. The personal computer is constantly maturing into a tool that extends our reach and our voice. I can send Christmas cards to 5 or 50 people immediately. I can author and print a beautiful mini-book from my home office. I have more choices with my media, but less time. How can I get the effectiveness of a traditional memory album along with the advantages of multimedia?

These are the dilemmas that face anyone with a camera, a PC, and a little motivation: How will you—

> **Manage your media**

> **Author your events**

> **Distribute them "anywhere"**

> **Do it quickly**

If you buy a digital camera, you'll shoot a lot of images. If you copy them to your computer, they will reside somewhere on your personal computer. Soon you will be swimming in pictures.

That's the problem. The technology has given us the freedom to freely choose which photos we keep or delete, but currently it's really difficult to author those images into an organized index. Digital cameras increase in capacity, as will the size of your hard drive. What will make you a better author and distributor of those memories?

If the technology allows us to do one thing, it will be to tell those stories currently untold.

The future of our memories will be influenced by the progressions of technology. The role it will play in our lives will be significant, and our memories aren't to be taken lightly. If you apply these key principles to your memory making now, they will continue to serve you well into the future:

> **Centralize:** Your process will need to be centralized to fit your needs. Someone (or something) will need to capture, author, and manage all of the images, dates, and stories. A central location will help you better prepare, document, and share your memories through a common process.

> **Digitize:** Your images will increasingly rely on being stored and delivered digitally—you will need an awareness to better organize and deliver your stories based on time, location, size, and format.

> **Benefit from lower cost for increased space:** The cost of digital storage will continue to go down; therefore, you will tell more stories to more people. Your untold stories today will become some of the most interesting and provoking memories to come.

> **Identify and extend your social network:** Your memories will be viewed by a multitude of people in a variety of locations. It's not just the album on the mantle anymore. The presentation and distribution of your memories will be formatted specifically for a specific viewer.

> **Be comfortably secure:** Your comfort should be in your control. Secure digital media will vary based on content type and delivery. As with all digital media, your privacy and security will be increasingly important to fend off viruses, piracy, copyright infringement, and identity theft.

About **This Book**

This is not a "How-To" book about software; rather, it is a "How-To" approach for more effective memory making.

This book *is* about empowering you to be more effective in preparing, documenting, and sharing your memories. The book will supply examples, instruction, and inspiration for action.

The book is designed to be referenced, browsed, or read in any order that suits you. It is organized into four major sections incorporating the fundamental pillars to personal memory creation.

> **Section 1:** You Have a Story To Tell. Let's Go! This section of the book speaks to the author in you. It will help you organize your approach and personalize your style.

> **Section 2:** More Effective Images   This section speaks to the photographer in you. It will present a practical approach to taking more effective images.

> **Section 3:** Organizing Your Living Library   This section speaks to the "shop-keeper" in you. This is your own personalized space where you organize, store, and retrieve all of your images and personal media. This section will help you better organize, edit, and retrieve the valuable mess that you call "your pictures."

> **Section 4:** Sharing Your Memories   This section speaks to the untold stories in you. It should help you extend your reach and your audience for what will become a body of work that you craft, author, and share.

The events that you document now and in the future take place in an increasingly digital and networked world.

This book is very visual for a reason. It is designed to show by example and share many professional and personal experiences of those who have contributed to their own memory making. This is not a "How-To" book about software; rather, it is a "How-To" approach for more effective memory making.

It is my wish that this book finds you well as you build a body of work that will become the legacy of stories you build and share.

Enjoy.

Dane M. Howard

dane m. howard
designer & father

section 1

You Have a Story to Tell. Let's Go!

> **Getting Started**

> **Working Quickly**

> **Choosing a Context**

> **Documentary Style**

> **The Basics: Story Stick Figures**

> **The Events Around You**

"I've been a professional designer for 12 years…

I've been a daddy for three…

and I tell stories all the time."

"My parents just got online…"

"We just bought a new digital camera…"

"We just took all these great pictures from our vacation…"

"I have all these images on my computer…"

"I just bought a new Media PC…"

"I want to build a scrapbook…"

"I want to tell better stories…"

Getting **Started**

You've got a really cool camera and a monster-sized hard drive. More often than not, you're stuck with a couple of gadgets and a little software, and then you are thrown into a very technical world of trying to figure out how to share your photographs. Is it really this hard? I used to think so…but it's really not.

Now what do I do?

Here's a roadmap:

> Ask the right questions.

> Find your audience.

> Work quickly.

> Choose a context.

> Author while you browse.

> Begin now.

One of the hardest things to do is to get started. Jumping into a context (or time frame) may be difficult. A timeline interface (top left) from Adobe Photoshop Album gives you access to your images indexed automatically by time. The software will automatically organize your images based on the time and date stamp already located in the image.

One day at a time...

A body of work is built in pieces. Think about the small things you can do already. If you've ever kept a journal, you know that the "daily entry" by itself isn't that stunning. It's when the series of days, weeks, and months come together to tell the bigger story. Realize that documenting the events of your life and those around you will become a body of work. Take small steps first, get comfortable, and then take on larger projects.

> **Write an e-mail...to yourself.** Use this existing daily habit to capture notes to yourself about photos or recent memories you've had. Use the mail as a reference later.

> **Schedule a meeting...for yourself.** Set aside a 30-minute slot at least twice a week. Give yourself some time to browse your photos and group them together.

> **Browse/group photos.** When you copy your photos, do you look at them? Try to group them by category or isolate duplicates of some of your favorite groups. Come back to them later to edit and share.

A daily routine can generate a body of work before you know it. Ask yourself what you can do today as a natural part of your daily routine. Find a way to capture those efforts. A library program like Microsoft Digital Image Library is a great way to organize your memories.

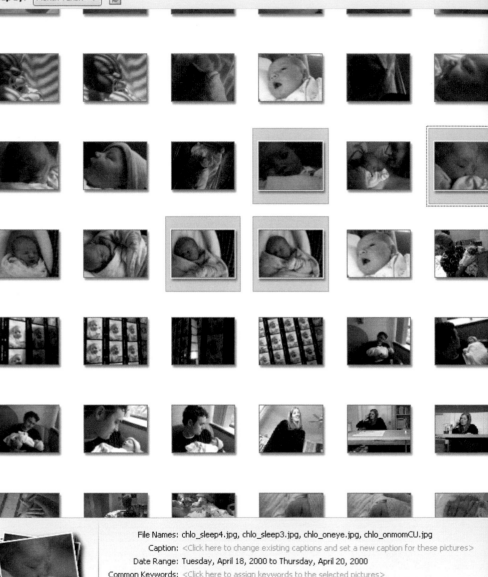

Ask the Right Questions

Be sure to ask yourself questions that will bring you towards your goal of personal memory creation. Soon you will have created a rich body of work. By asking the right questions, you should be able to choose the right audience for your memories and determine how to best author photos for them.

What do I do already?

being_a_dad.txt

A quick note next to your images will add context and flavor to your photos. You'll find it valuable when you reference the photo later, regardless of how you share it.

> What are my habits?

> What do I do (daily) already?

> What is the tone I'm looking for?

> Who is my main audience?

> What is the desired reaction I'm looking for?

> What do I want my body of work to look like?

> What do I already know?

> When will I most likely be shooting my photos?

> Where will I share them?

chloehoward.com

Where it all started...for me.

This is a place where it all started for me. I created a place where the events of my daughter's life became the basis for everything I was going to share. I decided that anything and everything was fair game. With a starting point (April 17, 2000) and a destination unknown, I used a simple timeline to help build the structure of our journey together.

My main audience was Chloe's grandparents. As time passed, we began to share our stories with extended family and friends. I discovered that I could easily direct the attention of a specific group of friends or family by e-mail. I would send them a link to a specific story (or series of stories) I had posted.

I found myself sending specific images and content by e-mail or by our digital picture frame. I invited guests to visit the site every couple of months.

My audience began to grow...

A simple index organized by time will give a natural structure to your body of work. Events can be dated and used as a reference point. In this case, Chloe's age is automatically calculated by the computer based on her birthdate.

2000   2001   2002   2003   2004   2005

Chloe // Current Age: 3 years, 3 months, 11 days, 19 hours, 11 minutes and 51 seconds.

Chloe Index //

①

Photos //

06/14/2003 // **Picking Berries:** A fun afternoon with grandma No-no and grandpa FD

06/14/2003 // **A Proud big Sister:** She mimics mommy and learns how to be "helpful".

04/27/2003 // **A birthday without the day:** We celebrate her third birthday in pieces of separate day

04/27/2003 // **Chalk drawings, sidewalk style:** fun with chalk

04/27/2003 // **Driveway: Blue chalk egg:** It reminded me of the 'simple' things. The way play probabl

04/19/2003 // **Egg-dye extravaganza:** We dyed some eggs for easter. super fun!

04/18/2003 // **Horsin' around w/ the Goehners:** a classic moment b/t two families with kids...

04/19/2003 // **Egg hunt & a lollipop:** 2 days after her surgery, she was looking for eggs and licking lo

04/17/2003 // **One Brave Day: (1)(2)(3)(4)(5)(6)(7):** Chloe gets surgery on her little foot.

04/05/2003 // **Daddy daughter weekend (1)(2)(3):** a day in the life of daddy & chloe...

04/05/2003 // **Party Balloons:** Fun with static electricity...

03/20/2003 // **Walk in the evening:** it was beautiful light...

03/20/2003 // **A _Fun_ Walk in the evening:** and a little attitude...

03/21/2003 // **Kick the bear:** This was so much fun.. we just had to do it again.

02/25/2003 // **Doggies and sunshine:** Simple as watching & learning...

01/02/2003 // **The Great Duo:** We happened to be just hanging out before bedtime...

Certain types of media (such as a Microsoft Plus! Digital Media Edition Photo Story movie) can be sent to specific friends or family who might benefit from a faster Internet connection.

Find **Your Audience**

A good question to start with is: Who really benefits from this body of work you are creating? Who are you really making this for? Is this going to be for yourself or your family and friends? Will you show this to your girlfriend or your child one day? Figure out who is going to be your primary audience and then plan to direct most of your energy to speak to what this audience needs.

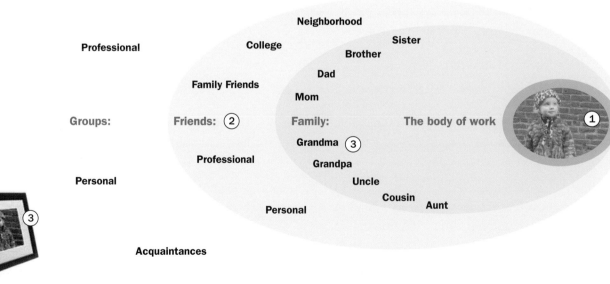

Colleagues

Neighborhood

Professional

College   Sister

Brother

Family Friends   Dad

Mom

Groups: Friends: ②   Family: The body of work   ①

Grandma ③

Professional   Grandpa

Personal   Uncle

Cousin   Aunt

Personal

Acquaintances

The grandparents receive a customized experience through a digital picture frame (www.ceiva.com). Pictures are sent directly to the frame automatically from an account we've set up.

13

Force yourself to...

Work Quickly...

Working quickly will force you to make decisions quickly. It will consequently keep your images more authentic.

This is a good thing.

By documenting and sharing your images quickly, you'll force yourself to "get out of the way" of the process and find a path (method) of least resistance. This is an important path to discover because it will expose a way of working that you can build upon and optimize for when you're crunched for time (which is usually the case). Early on, I found a couple of methods I liked to use. Over the years, I've optimized my technique to increase my efficiency. If you can get over the mental roadblocks, you'll be quickly on your way to building a habit of sharing and logging your images. Working quickly forces you to make decisions quickly. Here are some steps I use when posting to my website:

(1) **Browse and Grab.** Grab 5–10 photos. Look for a narrative angle and for a visually compelling sequence. Start to think about writing captions that give context to these images. I try to find a series of photos that speak to a particular context or story that means something to me at that moment.

(2) **Edit and Optimize.** Get the photos "ready" for publishing. Bring them into Adobe Photoshop or Microsoft Digital Image Pro for some quick cropping, color correction, and resizing. Output them to a width and height that your HTML template accommodates well. If I'm not in the mood for tweaking, sometimes I'll just resize the photos for the templates.

This is the fastest and quickest "manual" process for me. I have since automated a few steps, but the basic steps are the same, even with an integrated piece of software.

(3) **Batch Rename.** To make sure all your images fit well into their new folder, name them all simply and sequentially so that the HTML file will pick them up automatically. I call my files 1.jpg, 2.jpg, 3.jpg, and so on…because my HTML template looks for files with these names.

(4) **Duplicate and Edit the Page.** Duplicate the file structure from a previous story, and rename the new folder. Next, in a simple HTML editor (Microsoft FrontPage, Macromedia Dreamweaver, or even Microsoft Word), edit the page relative to the new context. Just edit the caption text. I keep it simple and then save the document. I don't rename anything except the folder that the new files are located in.

(5) **Update the Index.** Add the new context to your index, add the link to the story, and save the index page.

(6) **Publish (Post the Files).** After a quick test in a browser, upload the new folder containing the HTML page with folder and updated index page. I check the page online for broken links, and then I'm done.

2000

2001

2002

2003

I keep a simple index (spine) organized by time. Any new story (rib) is represented by a folder with its associated media. The navigation quickly returns to the index.

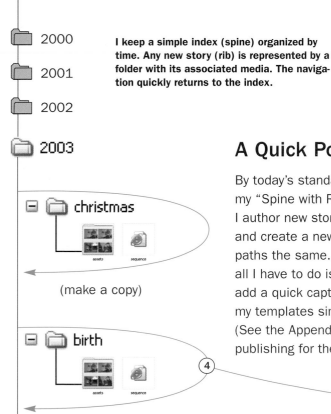

christmas

assets   sequence

(make a copy)

birth

assets   sequence

④

A Quick Posting

By today's standards, I keep a pretty simple website. I call it my "Spine with Ribs" model (described on page 38). When I author new stories for the web, I like to duplicate my folder and create a new folder based on the date. I keep all the paths the same. When I insert new photos into the template, all I have to do is batch optimize and rename them. I can add a quick caption to the page and I'm done. I try to keep my templates simple and my images in an adjacent folder. (See the Appendix, for more information on web logging and publishing for the web.)

⑤ 04.17.00

index :: date

image1.jpg   image2.jpg   image3.jpg   etc.

caption text to accompany event

⑥

<u>NY in Style!</u>: Being cool in NY!

<u>Perfect Center Piece</u>: Eat your heart

<u>NY: Empire State Building</u>: 86 floors

<u>2 month shots :(</u> Chloe gets her 3 mont

...ake of Purpl

...hloe learns

...ew face she

...ss who's w

...nts she look

...ena visit

...'re a family!

...Katelyn and

...Today it'll be green**: A fashion show: c

<u>Yellow Suits and Grandpa Gayle:</u>

<u>Bath Time!</u> An afternoon bath is good for

<u>Things that are beautiful</u> Flowers blo

<u>Day 2: Recovery & Discovery</u> Both

<u>The Birth!</u> She was so alert, so with it. S

<u>The Birth // part 2:</u> images that made a

<u>The Nursery</u> They make baby stuff for e

<u>Our niece, Katelyn</u> The images from h

4/17/2000 - 36 items

image4.jpg   image3.jpg

View Picture...
Batch Edit Pictures in Mini Lab... ②
Send in E-mail...
Print...

Rotate Clockwise
Rotate Counterclockwise

Convert File Format...
Edit Keywords...

Cut
Copy
Delete
Rename ③
Properties...

①

image1.jpg   image2.jpg

Much of this sequence was shot by placing the camera on the ground. I decided to open and close the sequence with similar shots of Chloe leading off the frame in different directions. This gave me some visual bookends to focus on her mobility. It was relevant since she was recovering from foot surgery just three days prior.

"We happened to be the popular chalk space that day." And the kids from across the street began to come on over. Chloe was super interested in the chalk. She had just gotten out of her surgery a couple days earlier and was ready to be outside. We put some old sweats on her, and she crawled around until the pant on her cast leg had a hole in the knee. At one point, she played with the blue little chalk egg for about 30 minutes as she went up and down the driveway, pushing the egg up and throwing it down the driveway. I think she would still be doing it if I hadn't pulled her in for dinner...

The textured sidewalk in juxtaposition to the worn sock brings a new context to the piece. The use of scale also brings some visual balance and cadence to the sequence.

What happened next? An intentional cropping and composition choice places her crawling off to the side of the page. This might suggest that the sidewalk story continued. You can create intentional edits that solicit more interest just by making a simple cropping choice.

Choose a Context

Context will give your images a point of reference. Choose images that build naturally on some type of context. You can document and share the context of the images now, or you can prepare it for a later opportunity.

Choosing a context is a great approach to take when it comes to shooting pictures and organizing them. It's a way to plan stories and group common occurrences. I do this all the time when I shoot pictures because it gives me an "assignment" while shooting. I also use the technique when I'm staring at about 100 pictures, and I need to put them into a cohesive sequence.

A context can be just about anything…

< Pet smells, abstract shapes, Buildings I like, Cloud shapes, Close-up on shoes, vacation breakfasts, car trips — scenes from my window, Dad's favorite chair, **Chalk drawings**, Yellow outfits, Great flowers, scenes in Mirrors, Pets in my neighborhood, Shadows in my backyard, birds-eye views, baseball jerseys, Worm's-eye views, The hands of our family, Chloe's favorite toys, The video box collection, Bike (details), bedspread patterns, The kid's "sippy" cups, our Morning rituals, A walk in the Park, A really fun slide, Grandpa's chores, Favorite documents >

Chalk Drawings, Sidewalk Style

Context: Fun with Chalk…

Sometimes you don't choose your context; it chooses you. One day, we happened to be the popular "chalk" space in the neighborhood. My story was about nothing in particular. I just wanted to document the texture and the light. What I discovered was a whole new point of view when I was that close to the ground.

This was a moment that just happened upon us. I sat back and just watched it happen…with my camera, of course.

It's perfectly OK to choose a context that is simple. It will be a focal point for your narrative and will guide your selection process.

17

I read that a shop owner in New Jersey took his camera out every morning before he opened his shop. He used the same camera and tripod every day. He placed the camera in the exact spot, every morning.

He owned the shop for 20 years.

It wasn't the shop that became popular; it was the body of work that he had produced over those 20 years. Keeping the context simple will allow you to document how things change.

SHOWING CHANGE IS A SIMPLE FORM OF NARRATIVE.

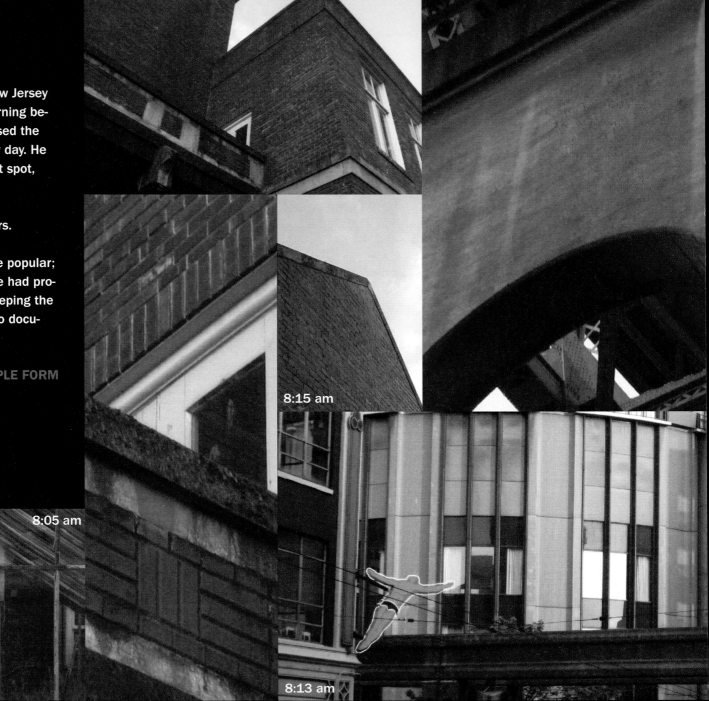

8:17 am

8:27 am

8:15 am

8:05 am

8:13 am

CHOOSE SOMETHING REALLY SPECIFIC, AND DON'T THINK ABOUT IT TOO MUCH.

When you choose a context, remember that there are no rules. You can take this principle and choose anything you like. Here are a few of my favorite topics:

> **Time:** Time has a lot of interesting aspects to it. It can be extended or compressed. Time can also be scheduled and planned for. You can set up any increment of time you like and document the events within those parameters. If you log your images by time of day, you'll have a built-in structure to carry your story. Be sure to choose a context within your own "time." Try "play time" or "lunch time" or "practice time"—you'll find characteristics in the day that you've never noticed before. The similarities will fascinate you, and so will the differences. A context makes for good stories and good image sequences. Once you've discovered "lunch time" with a camera, force yourself to document it with something different, like an audio recorder or by writing it down. You'll discover new things that you hadn't noticed before.

> **Color:** Colors are everywhere. They're an easy context to choose and create surprisingly great results. Why? Continuity. When you do a series of images based on color, all of the images seem to work better juxtaposed to each other. This is a great way to create continuity and discover hidden narratives. I discovered black and white. I also started to notice that patterns on a lot of baby toys are high-contrast. I did a couple of series on baby toys. "Black and White" became the context. Another series I did was based on which sleeper my daughter was wearing. All I did was photograph her when she was in these different sleepers. "Pink" became one of my favorites, and so was "purple."

> **Perspective:** Choosing a specific camera angle or perspective can be a great context choice for a narrative. Low angles or ground shots give you the same point of view on all your subjects. By focusing on the angle of the camera or the location and direction the camera is pointed, you can direct the opportunities that present themselves. With a similar perspective you get complementary angles and view planes. You can use these compositions to build and edit your images into a cohesive series. The series also gives you an opportunity to focus. Look for similar patterns in light or perspective, or focus on the differences and create a story of displacement and contrast.

> **Objects:** Another great context is to place your subject with or near a specific object or person. You'd be surprised how much fun "10 minutes with a hairbrush" or "rose bush" can be. This sounds silly, but it's really fun. What you'll soon discover is the variety in your photographs once you start shooting this way. Your images won't look the same, and you'll begin to notice all the subtle expressions that make discovery so special.

COHESIVE
IMAGES =
COHESIVE STORY

No matter what you decide to document, find a context that grabs you. Once you've found it, play with multiple perspectives—that will make it interesting. You'll find a wealth of things to share.

Microsoft Digital Image Library is a great way to browse your photos, allowing you to select, edit, and author quickly and easily.

(1) A Quick Photo Story:
Sometimes the quicker you can author a piece of media, the better. Even when you're browsing media, you can author a quick story. I find that I benefit from this "wizard-like" authoring because it can remind me to tell a bigger story later or just keep it quick and fresh. (See next page for details.)

(2) An E-Mail to Mom:
An e-mail like this is very quick to author. Be sure to CC yourself, so you'll have a record of context and the content to reference later. Capturing your thoughts when you have them is a valuable first step to authoring.

Author **While You Browse**

Many times, we try to organize all of our old images, smiling and remembering as we go. **I've found that if I can capture and edit my thoughts while I'm browsing, I create an opportunity to craft and document those little memories as I go.** Don't confuse browsing with authoring. You can easily spend a lot of time browsing through images with no intent to share or create a new context. But if you can keep a folder, bin, or concept fresh while you're browsing, you can quickly add a number of images and quick notes. Before you know it, you'll be able to look into that bin and find 8 or 10 jumping-off points to quickly write about and share.

You can get completely sidetracked by the technical details of the process. However, I have found that when I document something fresh, I naturally begin to create a context for it from the event(s) that preceded it. Technical details that are involved emerge as I move through the process.

The first step in authoring is the creation of temporary image "bins." Use them to store copies of the images that you want to incorporate into a story later.

Using Microsoft Plus! Digital Media Edition Photo Story
Much More Than the "Keeper"

Here is a classic scene. The family portrait… Many times we rarely see this many photos in context, but it illustrates an important point: **There is more to the story than just the keeper.** This is where a program like Plus! Photo Story comes along. This little program is a run-away hit. This wizard-like interface by Microsoft allows you group photos into a seemingly rich presentation with music and narration. The output is a .wmv movie file, so it is easily transportable. You can add audio to photos in your own voice to add flavor or context to the scene. Now you can send the keeper *and* provide a richer context. Most of the time the extra side stories are more interesting, anyway. You learn more about the people and who they are.

"When we sat around the dinner table, we didn't talk about the portrait. We laughed about the things we did. That's what I remember."

Plus! Photo Story offers quite a bit control over the timing and movement of the images. With the Plus! edition, you get an advanced tab that gives you control over the timing and cadence of your story.

⊙ Archive   🖼 Create a Photo Story   🖂 Send in E-mail   🔖 Keywords

up By: Date Taken ▾   ⟳ | Create a story with pictures, music, and narration. |

1   When you begin your story, you'll want to think about the image selection and juxtapositions they will have. This is basic image editing. Don't just live with the order that happens when the images are imported. Mix up the close-up shots with those that are farther away. This will create a natural visual cadence to your story.

2   **Timing and Preview:** After importing and re-ordering, you can quickly preview your sequence and adjust the timing using the advanced features. You can also add narration on select images by pressing the red record button.

Configure Microphone…

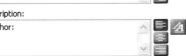

☑ Add a title page to your story

Title:

| Type a title |

Description:

| Author: |

Number of seconds to display title page:

| 5 ⇕ | seconds

☐ Add a background image on the title page

3   **Title Page and Description:** Use this to add an introduction or "chapter-like" feel to your piece. If authoring multiple stories, you might want to set them apart in this way.

The value of the nonkeeper is evident here. We know more about this family by including the images that reveal the story behind the story of this simple family portrait. Look for the not-so-obvious in your sequences. Chances are that you'll remember the moments, not the images.

4

Ambience and Final Preview: This step gives you a chance to "sweeten" the story with a piece of music or other audio. View a final preview before you output it.

5

Output Final Story: You can control the output and resolution of the story before it is saved.

BEHIND THE SCENES

A good Plus! Photo Story can even replace the traditional "keeper." Reward your audience with a rare perspective. This will add to the authenticity and intimacy of the overall sequence. Use some of your "leftovers"—you'll be surprised how rich in narrative they will appear.

23

My First Real Story

Jumping In…

Shooting and editing in a documentary style means to begin "right now." Don't try to remember what happened a month ago, and don't try to predict what will happen, just try to focus on trying to document what is happening right now.

When my daughter was born, I just had to jump in. I had made myself an ambitious goal. I wanted my friends and family to wake up the morning after she was born and see a link to our website in their e-mail inboxes. It was my goal to bring the immediacy and the intimacy as close as possible to those who could not be there. I wanted them to share the feelings close to the time that we had felt them.

I gave myself two hours to tell that story. I was enthusiastically trying to document the entire day of events as it was fresh in my mind. I started by choosing my first image. ① I couldn't believe I was looking at imagery so quickly after those events had occurred. I began to remember the events of the day.… What came through when I reviewed the images was the body language my wife showed through her hands. It was beautiful. ② I began to remember the gestures, the equipment, and the "language" of the hospital. ③ I decided to illustrate our day by building off a few shots I had taken of her hands and then juxtaposing that to the data that measured exactly what I was looking at. Of course there is always a payoff. ④

The most significant achievement (for me) was the ability to quickly get out of the way of the material and focus on the speed and authenticity of what I was feeling when I sent that story. Now, more than three years later, when I look at that sequence, I realize that I would not have done anything differently. For me, the authenticity and immediacy of the images were most important to capturing the event.

In this case, less was more…

Establish who it is and where it is happening. In this sequence, a simple choice of imagery can establish a setting and an emotion. My audience knew the context of what was happening. I wanted to remind them of the personal journey.

Using scale. These two shots in sequence can illustrate the power and strength of what is happening without disclosing too much. Using eyes and hands can be powerful narrative tools. They also introduce a visual element of scale and intimacy through their close association with the subject.

All of it.

Go to album // Birth
Go to Chloe // Index

Pacing and the payoff. The image of the equipment was an element of perspective that I felt is oftentimes overlooked. The payoff is a tightly cropped image of an intimate moment. Cropping was critical to the effectiveness of the image.

Begin **Now**

Take your camera and shoot a series on anything you like. Try to share this series with five of your closest friends or family. Send it to yourself as well. Try to do this as quickly and effortlessly as you can. You can use any means of communication you like, using any and all software or techniques that you feel comfortable with.

I SUGGEST THAT YOU PICK UP YOUR CAMERA AND DOCUMENT SOMETHING THAT YOU ARE DOING RIGHT NOW.

When you've documented something, ask yourself two important questions:

Were you effective? Were you satisfied with the images and the story you told? Did it communicate what you intended? Did it effectively communicate to the audience you intended? More important, would you have been glad to be on the receiving end of this? If you were to reference it later, is there a clear indication of when this event occurred and/or was published?

Were you efficient? How long did it take you from beginning to end? Did you try and tell too much or did you not tell enough? What part of the process was bogging you down? Did you feel like you had the right equipment, software, or skills necessary to accomplish what you wanted? Was your idea great, but your approach not so great? Did you understand all the steps you needed to take? Write down (specifically) which steps held you up.

A Project to Get You Started

Here is a quick exercise to get you thinking about a process and an audience that matters most to you. Use one (or all) of these delivery methods so that you'll ask the right questions when developing your own process of sharing images. This is valuable to not only expose what you do know, but more important, what you don't.

Take a minute and think about your authoring process.

Part 1: Document Your Images

1 Shoot five new photos (minimum) of a subject or an event that interests you.

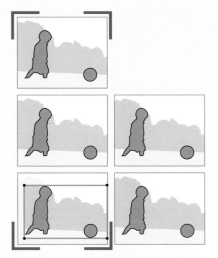

2 Edit those photos down to three. (Why three? It's easier than one, yet gives you a natural narrative structure to work with.)

3 Crop, rotate, and sequence those images to best represent the "essence" of what you are trying to communicate.

Part 2: Author Your Images

4 Arrange these three photos in a sequence or layout that fits your concept.

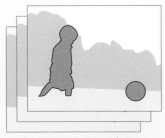

5 Write a brief caption to describe the series. (Add a time/date stamp and brief context.)

caption text to accompany images

Part 3: Share with Your Audience

Once you've authored your images, choose one of the following delivery methods to share with your five chosen friends:

body text to accompany email

AN E-MAIL (OR INSTANT MESSAGE) ATTACHMENT

1. **Attach the images to a new e-mail (or instant message).**
2. **Write your caption(s) to accompany the message.**
3. **Address the e-mail message with the appropriate recipients.**
4. **Send it to your five chosen friends and family members.**

Be sure to note anything that would improve your effectiveness, timeliness, or efficiency.

index :: date

image1.jpg **image2.jpg** **image3.jpg**

caption text to accompany images

A WEB PAGE POSTING

1. **Resize the images to a "web-appropriate" file size (try 640 × 480).**
2. **Build the web page layout to accommodate three images and a caption.**
3. **Choose a color and font for the page.**
4. **Save the web page and its image files.**
5. **Upload/post the new files to an online web server.**
6. **Distribute/share the new link to your five chosen friends and family members.**

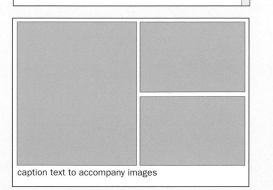

caption text to accompany images

A COLOR PRINTOUT

1. **Import your photos into a document you feel comfortable printing.**
2. **Write your caption(s) to accompany the images.**
3. **Arrange the photos in the document to fit your desired concept.**
4. **Print the document to a local printer or service.**
5. **Share the prints with your five chosen friends and family members.**

How did you do?

THE STORY OF A LOUD BAND

Oxbow is a noise rock art band from San Francisco that puts on a blistering live show mixing intense musicianship with performance art. To tour without major label support, the band and their manager put together as many gigs as they can and then make the rest up as they go.

My goal was to make a documentary film that captured both the power of Oxbow's live performances and the commitment it takes to tour as an independent band.

—Christian Anthony

Documentary **Style**

When you find your audience, you'll need a method that allows you to take better pictures, organize them more efficiently, and share them effectively.

This takes a little preparation and the right approach.

*This was my first film and I was a crew of one, so my strategy was to always have a **still camera** with me when not shooting video.*

On tour with a band named Oxbow. These photos were taken over a four-week period while the band toured through Germany, Norway, England, and Belgium.

If there has been anything I've learned over the years, it's that you can always learn to tell better stories! Your audience will change, and so will you. Any emotion can be produced by your guiding voice. A reflection of yourself can be crafted into the stories you tell.

Because I was using a digital camera, I shot upwards of 50 photos a day to capture as much of the experience as possible to give me greater flexibility when editing. When you consistently take that many pictures, your eye begins to sharpen and you start to see the pictures that articulate the mood of each experience.

Documentary Style **Defined**

So how do you document the life of your children, your hobbies, or passions? Where do you start? There really are no rules, only guidelines.

Take time to observe. You'll need to combine a lot of yourself, your perspective, and the tools that you have available to make it happen. There are remarkable moments that happen around you all the time. You've always heard that great photographers carry their cameras with them. In a way, all you have to do is bring the camera with you when you carry your briefcase, backpack, diaper bag, purse, or phone. The little candid moments you capture bring people closer to your life.

The documentary style that we know today has been shaped by filmmakers, photographers, and storytellers. It's both an art form and an approach for capturing life's moments as close to their original form as possible. It's difficult to explain what makes a story effective, but you should keep three key principles in mind when telling these stories in a documentary style:

> **Immediacy:** The visual language of "now."

> **Intimacy:** Those things that bring us emotionally closer.

> **Authenticity:** How genuine is your "voice"?

When we document our memories, we save pieces of ourselves.

Immediacy

What is happening "right now"? This is what keeps your audience interested and coming back. Keeping your relatives and friends up-to-date on what is happening with you, your child, or your life will pull them into the stories of what you are experiencing. If at all possible, don't wait to put up pictures of events that happened three months ago on the website after you've already sent out prints! Think about ways to use the immediacy of the Internet and wireless technologies and how to take full advantage of "no time zones." Thinking about these things will bring visitors back and even keep them wanting more! Understand that you're not necessarily going for a lot of traffic, but that you are interested in people spending quality time there. If you are sensitive to the timeliness of your information, you will be rewarded by loyal visitors. There is a line (a fine one) between an interested audience and an annoyed audience. You have to find the balance. Grandma can't get enough, but your friends at work are saying enough already. Find the right medium for your audience to define immediacy.

Examples: consider a website, a digital picture frame, e-mail, or instant messaging. Consider the tradeoff between constant updates versus less timely, yet media-rich presentations. Images that are presented in close succession create an immediacy, which draws your audience closer. When possible, find ways to automate your process (such as using a web cam or image droplets).

There is a visual language of "Now," and then there is the practice of delivering it... FAST.

August 12, 2003

Timestamps and motion blur play an active role in helping to communicate immediacy. The image quality (and presentation) contribute to how immediate it feels. A date stamp will immediately give context. Use this to your advantage for those events that "just" happened.

Intimacy

Sharing your beloved memories with others is an intimate act in itself, but the following principles will make your stories even more intimate:

> **Intimate photographs produce intimate stories.** Editing and cropping your photographs effectively will produce more compelling stories. Sometimes one image will say it all. Take close-up pictures of the eyes and hands. Don't say too much. Let the image speak. On the day my wife gave birth to our daughter, there was no way I was going to show my wife actually "having" the baby, but I was with her while she was in labor. I took just a few shots of her and her surroundings. I showed a close-up of her hands, clenched fists of pain, and another of the monitor showing the contractions. Those images told the whole story. It was an intimate moment in which you felt her pain and you were with her. Intimacy is elusive and personal. What touches one person won't have the same effect on another. If it touches you, it might speak to someone else.

> **Take chances.** It takes courage to walk up to a stranger and make new friends. It also takes courage to tell a sad or difficult story. Our daughter was born with a clubfoot. A lot of people would ask about it and wonder about its severity. Still others didn't even know what a clubfoot was. This gave us an opportunity to talk about it, discuss how we felt, and discuss how the doctors fixed it. One story became two. Those two became the premise to two other stories. The result was a series of intimate stories that kept our family and friends close to us during a difficult time. The added support surrounding those events was priceless. It happened only because I took a chance.

THE GOOD AND THE BAD

I rarely see albums with images that show difficult or hard times. We tend to edit out those stories that make us grow and remind us of how lucky we are.

Eyes and hands are some of the the most intimate attributes of a subject.

This was a difficult story for me to tell. It is one that I will always remember and that I want to share with my daughter when she is older. For us, it is the hard times we experience that make the good that much better.

Authenticity

An authentic image is key to keeping a story honest. Don't art-direct your visual presentations too much. Here's why: if you think about the first two principles (immediacy and intimacy), anything you do to dress them up takes them further away from their original form.

Every time an image is colorized, resized, or placed within a colored border, it becomes less authentic.

There's something important about the extra-visual language that surrounds certain types of visual information. Whether it's the appearance of an e-mail message, a digital image, or a 35mm print, be mindful of your media's source and how the visual elements within the image contribute to its authenticity.

I recommend filling your presentations with 95% content and 5% frame.

You don't leave the art museum talking about the frames.

The content is the most important part and is the source of your story.

Our eyes can quickly identify inauthentic elements. An image that is touched up is clearly recognizable. Any emotion evident in the original photograph is now competing with the treatment forced by the context of the frame and color choice. These types of treatments move the photograph away from being genuine and intimate. The visual language that's created is more decorative than narrative.

Three **Key Principles…**

When documenting a chosen subject, here are three key principles
to keep in mind to improve your narrative:

> **Get Closer.** I'll give you a secret to creating intimate portraits. It can be summed up in two words: Get close. The chances of you producing better images will increase if you get closer to your subjects and then focus on these areas. This works for still-life photography as well.

By getting closer, you force both perspective and focus. There's an optical phenomenon that occurs when a camera's focal length is shortened. You get an effect called *selective focus*. You maximize the contrast between those elements in focus and those out of focus. Getting closer to your subjects will naturally produce more interesting compositions and intimate opportunities in your images.

> **Be Flexible.** Get ready for the unexpected. You'd better get used to this if you're a parent, too. If you set out to do one thing, be perfectly comfortable if something else happens. One way to completely liberate you from expectations is to stop looking through the viewfinder on your camera. I hold the camera out and just start shooting. I waste a lot of images this way, but with the digital camera, I just erase the bad ones on the spot. Don't feel like you can't make any mistakes. Who's going to know? Some of my favorite images are the ones I thought I'd messed up.

> **Move Around.** This is all about variety and moving around the material. A camera flattens a three-dimensional space and creates a two-dimensional slice of a view. Sometimes I imagine that I'm cutting a diamond, and the perfect image will be seen in one of the facets that I create. Move your view plane drastically and effectively to generate unforeseen views and hidden light. Any story can be seen from multiple viewpoints. Use this concept to your advantage. A little work on your part will greatly increase your enjoyment when you review your images later.

WHEN I FAIL

When my pictures are looking really stale, I look at my feet. I see if they are moving. If i'm standing still, I'm not working hard enough.

The Basics: **Story Stick Figures**

When you think about writing a "story," it's a little intimidating. Instead, think about building a body of work in pieces. This is where the metaphor of a stick figure works for me. The simple shapes should represent the simple pieces of a greater whole. A body of work is not a masterpiece, but rather a series of strokes.

The Big Picture

You should think about a statement that defines your body of work. This statement should be your compass, essentially your global north. The big picture is really about the metastory or the topic of your entire body of work. It should be easy to say and easy to remember. Try making a statement such as:

"THIS BODY OF WORK:

...is a website that documents the life of my daughter.

or

...is my entire collection of antique bird houses.

or

...covers the events of our relationship."

A statement like this will keep you thinking about the big picture. The details of the events you author will be significant, but the body of work will strengthen by a cohesive mission or statement that you create.

Photos //
08/29/2003 //
08/14/2003 //
08/14/2003 //
04/27/2003 //
04/27/2003 //
04/27/2003 //
04/19/2003 //
04/18/2003 //
04/19/2003 //
04/17/2003 //
04/05/2003 //
04/05/2003 //
03/20/2003 //
03/20/2003 //
03/21/2003 //
02/25/2003 //
01/02/2003 //

01/29/2003 //
01/26/2003 //
01/28/2003 //
01/25/2003 //
12/31/2002 //
12/14/2002 //
12/24/2002 //
12/24/2002 //
01/03/2003 //

When I built my daughter's website, my statement of purpose was simply "The life and events of my daughter"—which I indexed by using a central theme (time).

There is a lot of formal documentation on narrative structure, but that is for the "pros." I just want to share my pictures wth you. Here's something simple…

The old Vinyl: Chloe is introduced to how music used to be played…

Picking Berries: A fun afternoon with grandma No-no and grandpa FD

A Proud big Sister: She mimicks mommy and learns how to be "helpful".

A birthday without the day: We celebrate her third birthday in pieces of separate days..

Chalk drawings, sidewalk style: fun with chalk

Driveway: Blue chalk egg: It reminded me of the 'simple' things. The way play probably used to be.

Egg-dye extravaganza: We dyed some eggs for easter. super fun!

Horsin' around w/ the Goehners: a classic moment b/t two families with kids…

Egg hunt & a lolli-pop: 2 days after her surgery, she was looking for eggs and licking lolli-pops..

One Brave Day: (1)(2)(3)(4)(5)(6)(7): Chloe gets surgery on her little foot.

Daddy daughter weekend (1)(2)(3): a day in the life of daddy & chloe…

Party Balloons: Fun with static electricity…

Walk in the evening: it was beautiful light…

A Fun Walk in the evening: and a little attitude…

Kick the bear: This was so much fun.. we just had to do it again.

Doggies and sunshine: Simple as watching & learning…

The Great Duo: We happened to be just hanging out before bedtime…

A day in the snow: The girls went sledding with Diana…

Puzzles all the time: I can't believe how good she is…

Track #7: Just a little Faith…is all you need.

Early Morning hat: A hat and some blocks is all we need…

Contemplate '03: Chloe was thinking about what '03 would bring…

Gymnastics Class: An hour and a bunch of tumbles and tramps…

Twas the night before Christmas: and all through the house…

Christmas Eve: a quick photo with daddy and mommy

on Stage: waiting to sing her song…

① Engage

② Related Context

Once you have your narrative structure you can add your own color. Each addition you make to this body of work will give more definition and character to your album.

Building around a narrative context is like dressing up a stick figure. It starts off with a simple point of engagement. ① This is designed to pull the reader into the story and provide something compelling to read. A reader that's interested can make a conscious choice to read further into the related context and to explore. ② Context can be unified by a common timeline or index.

Structurally Speaking

A narrative structure can feel like a very esoteric thing. I've used a couple of analogies to help me understand the essence of what a narrative structure can look like. More important, it helps me think about how I might create certain types of narrative connections between my media and how I build the interaction between the memories.

Here are three of my favorites:

You can mix and match any of these narrative structures for yourself.

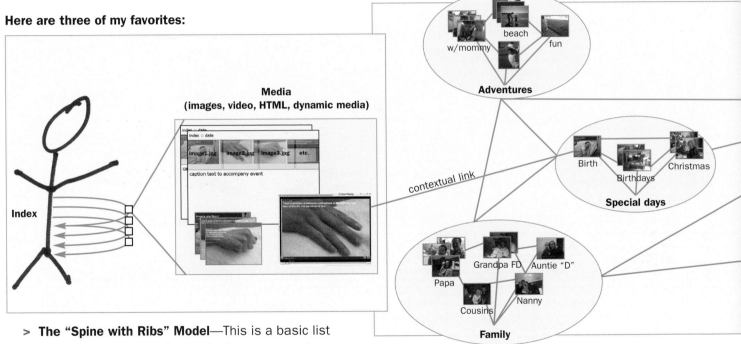

> **The "Spine with Ribs" Model**—This is a basic list with descriptive text. The "spine" represents the index organized by a central context (usually time) with links to specific media (the ribs). Each piece of media returns to the index, which provides a common navigational structure and facilitates interaction. In this model, you read stories in succession. The most frequently read story is prominently displayed.

> **The Bouquet Model**—These are contextual arrangements of related events or stories, usually organized by keyword (name, importance, media type, location, and so on). This contextual "fragrance" loosely binds the media together into contextual relationships that make the arrangements coherent. In this model, you read through related stories.

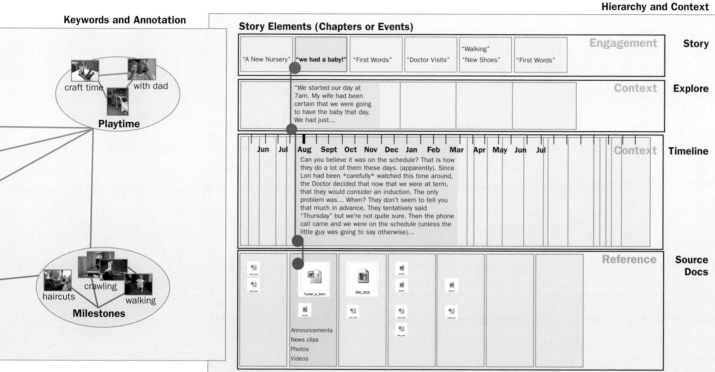

Keywords and Annotation

Playtime

craft time · with dad

Milestones

haircuts · crawling · walking

Hierarchy and Context

Story Elements (Chapters or Events)

"A New Nursery"	"we had a baby!"	"First Words"	"Doctor Visits"	"Walking" "New Shoes"	"First Words"

Engagement — **Story**

"We started our day at 7am. My wife had been certain that we were going to have the baby that day. We had just...

Context — **Explore**

Jun Jul **Aug** Sept Oct Nov Dec Jan Feb Mar Apr May Jun Jul

Can you believe it was on the schedule? That is how they do a lot of them these days. (apparently). Since Lori had been *carefully* watched this time around, the Doctor decided that now that we were at term, that they would consider an induction. The only problem was... When? They don't seem to tell you that much in advance. They tentatively said "Thursday" but we're not quite sure. Then the phone call came and we were on the schedule (unless the little guy was going to say otherwise)...

Context — **Timeline**

Tucker_is_born · IMG_0525

Announcements
News clips
Photos
Videos

Reference — **Source Docs**

I use the "Spine with Ribs" Model as the primary interface for my site.

I use the Bouquet Model for related stories and e-mail.

I use the Progressive Context Model for uniquely special events and significant stories when I have the time to create them.

I TIE IT ALL BACK TO AN INDEX SORTED BY TIME.

> **Progressive Context Model**—This narrative model was developed by Curtis Wong, a Microsoft researcher. This type of narrative structure presents a hierarchy with supporting context. The user can experience the narrative at any level of the hierarchy while remaining within context. Each level represents a distinct commitment from the audience to dive deeper and deeper into the narrative. In this model, users can freely traverse the model while maintaining context.

Crafting a Scene

To capture multiple images in alignment, place the camera on a table or other fixed surface. Take multiple exposures in the same location without moving the camera. The movement of your subject will be rendered in multiple images with a constant background. If you use this technique to register your images, you can usually hand-pick your favorite shot later in the computer and blend it into the desired image. Using this technique, you can even create an animation or a movie to show the essence of movement and to indicate time passing. This works very well for repetitive movements when used with a simple cross-dissolve.

When you use this technique, you get a picture-perfect image—a few pieces at a time. Here's how the technique was put to use:

1 Observation—With careful observation, the photographer lets the scene play out a bit, focusing on different parts of the scene. In this sequence of shots, he shoots different silhouettes of his wife and son next to the large shark tank.

2 Isolating the pieces—After he's captured the silhouettes, he snaps a few images with different placement of the fish in the tank. He plans to reconstruct the image later, and he could use "extra" fish in the scene.

3 Clone and assemble—While on the computer, he does the final composition by removing a glaring reflection and placing an "extra" into the shot on the right to balance the composition.

When you're capturing multiple images of the same scene, another great trick is to use video (such as Microsoft Plus! Photo Story or Microsoft Windows Movie Maker) to construct a simple and elegant playback of the scene. The displacement of the subjects in the frame illustrates the passing of time, giving you (the author) the ability to articulate the context and set the narrative.

Together we amassed more than 2000 photos. Strictly using film, this would have been an extremely costly venture.

Traveling: **The Events Around You**

The ongoing stories you present in your album will be limited only by what you choose to showcase. You are the author, director, photographer, and master of ceremonies all in one. The "album" you build will become a body of work before you know it. It will become the basis for memories that will be referenced for years to come. The sum of these memories will become the lifeblood of your community and the premise for the stories you share with your friends and your relatives. The investments you give your memories now will be strengthened by how well you document and contribute to that body of work. Above all, this process should be fun, and it will be.

If you think of your memories as a series of mini-events, the tasks become a little more manageable.

Think about what this experience feels like for others around you as you document and experience things together. I recently documented a trip to Europe with a long-time friend. It was fascinating to read some of his commentary on the photographs I took.

When traveling with others, you share experiences, yet see from very different perspectives. Use this to your advantage when sharing images and stories later.

Europe by Pictures, Memories by Themes
by William Lamb, Friend, Writer, Lawyer, & Uncle of Two

For five years, Dane and I had planned, cancelled, replanned and planned again to go to on a trip to Europe. As I sat in Charles de Gaulle airport waiting for Dane to stroll through the international arrival doors, I contemplated how we could capture the magnitude of this trip. How could we create memories that would not just represent visual attractions, but also a state of mind that all trips generate? A camera is an amazing tool, but would it be able to save more than just old buildings and history? Could it allow for more than just snapshots—could it capture the emotions and drama we felt in such a way that we could call it art? Our hope was to transform the common into the extraordinary—to show that our trip, even while visiting the typical sites, was anything but typical.

Together we amassed more than 2000 photos. Strictly using film, this would have been an extremely costly venture and probably impossible. With a digital camera, shooting excessively has no penalty. Dane photographed everything in sight and then photographed it again. But what was extraordinary about the photos was not the sheer number, but the perspective they provided: a unique encapsulation of our experience without seeming ordinary. The totality of the photos changed the traditional notions of vacation photography. What surfaced from the pictures was a more personal and compelling travel journal. I think what happens to most people on a trip is that they want to capture the "big moments": the Eiffel Tower, the Louvre, the Roman Coliseum, the Canals of Venice. But if you analyze your time spent on a vacation, the "big" moments comprise only maybe 5 percent of the trip. So when you get home and look at your pictures, you'll have a great many of the traditional tourist sites shot exactly like the postcards but not many of the images that truly represent the trip. Digital photography allows for a different approach.

Looking back over the photos, I can see huge **themes** that emerged.

Theme: Chocolate Croissant

This approach involves taking pictures in a manner that truly represents your experiences. Buy that Eiffel Tower postcard, but spend most of your time focusing on unique ways to record your travels that give your viewers a truer vision of what you experienced. **For example, my favorite photograph of my trip was one that Dane took after a hectic morning of shopping in Venice.** We had about thirty minutes to get to the train station. What I love about Europe is the pace at which things proceed and especially the pace experienced in the ritual of taking coffee in the morning. Dane and I had become obsessed with the simplicity of breakfast and how nothing could get in the way of this tradition. People might have been in a hurry, but if you watched the way they ate breakfast, you could never tell. We stopped for breakfast in a small café. There was nothing extraordinary about it; it looked like every local café all over Europe. We ordered the standard—espresso and a chocolate croissant. Before we sat down to eat—actually, stood to eat—Dane took a picture of the espresso and croissant. **This image captured more than just breakfast; it captured a theme of the trip if not a theme of Europe.** The picture was a reminder that there is no need to rush. We relaxed and ate breakfast.

We missed the train.

Caption: europe_2_023
Dimensions: 1152 x 864
Date Picture Taken: 8/17/2002 10:18 PM
Camera: Eastman Kodak Company DC210 Zoom (V03.10)
Size: 238 KB

Theme: Local Motion

Immediately following that shot came a pair of shots that further captured the essence of our trip. Dane set the camera on the counter and snapped a shot of the door simply by pressing the button—there was no focusing or looking through the viewfinder. He left the camera on the counter in the exact same location and snapped a shot 10 seconds later when a patron walked through the door. Viewing these two images gives one a sense of the constantly changing world we live in. Additionally, it provides a flavor of the local population. Often by capturing a local person in the most mundane of tasks, you can capture the feel and history of that place. Dane captured a moment of transition. Before this patron came through the door, it was Dane and I alone with the barista. When this gentleman came through the door, the place livened up with loud talking and laughter as patron and barista talked as if they were long-lost buddies. However, they had probably just seen each other the day before.

Theme: Blur

Another of my favorite photographs in this same theme also took place in Venice but at an entirely different establishment. This was an exclusive café with a very pricey menu. The wait staff was dressed to perfection. **The entire establishment exuded class.** Because it was afternoon and we were starting to fade, we ordered an espresso to revive us. **The place was extremely busy in preparation for the dinner rush.** We sat at the bar, and as Dane sipped his espresso with one hand, he took a picture with the other. The resulting image brilliantly captured the moment. The barista is out of focus because he was moving around rapidly doing five different things at once. The espresso saucer is at the forefront, crystal clear; **it shows that the espresso was too good to be put down.** Right there Dane captured more than a photo…

…he captured an experience and a feeling.

46

Theme: Table Settings

Other themes emerged from our trip. I think it is often the subtleties that separate cultures. Looking through our pictures, I notice an inordinate number of shots of table settings. Normally, you would think these mundane or common. But **a closer look shows that they are indicative of something unique to Europe:** they express the opposite of a fast food culture. Great care is taken in setting tables and preparing for meals. The vibrant white tablecloths often contrast with the surrounding scenery, making for extraordinary pictures. Similarly, **most European shopkeepers take meticulous care in displaying their wares.**

Perhaps the most interesting displays were of bottles of wine or olive oil arranged in almost geometric precision. Dane captured excellent shots of this art form. It is something that I took for granted when I saw it in person. But **it is a constant reminder of the fact that what may appear ordinary is often extraordinary.** So take the photo even if it seems mundane. You can always delete it, but more often than not, it will show a part of your journey that brings you back to a moment of sights, sounds, and smells that are uniquely representative of your trip.

Theme: The Louvre

One of the best photos from our Europe adventure combines both the table setting concept and the Louvre Museum. **If you have been to the Louvre, you know how overwhelming and exhausting it can be.** It is an endless labyrinth of the most impressive art and historical artifacts on earth. That alone is enough to tire you out, but when you add 50,000 very loud and boisterous art enthusiasts to navigate through, it starts to wear you down after only a few hours. So **we retreated to the courtyard and a small café.** It was a fantastic experience sitting watching the sunset over the Louvre and eating Caprese salad (made with tomato, fresh mozzarella, basil, and olive oil)—our staple throughout the trip. We stayed there for hours and **it was one of the most relaxing experiences on the trip.** Dane captured that experience by taking a shot through a wine glass that captured the Louvre, the table, and me all in a one frame. The composition of a photo often goes unnoticed. He could have easily taken a picture of the Louvre or me, but it would not have done justice to the moment. **In catching the entire moment through a wine glass, he added texture to the photo to frame a memorable afternoon.**

Theme: Food and Beverage

Europe overflows with good food and wine. Many of the most powerful images from our European trip centered around long meals and exquisite tastes. Everyday for three weeks I ate the same lunch—Caprese salad and bread. I couldn't stop. Sure, I ate other things, but I would always return to that colorful meal. Everywhere I went I would search for it. I remember in Cannes, we stopped at a small shop to buy our own raw materials in an attempt to replicate a fine dining experience. Let's just say it was not the same because most of my mozzarella landed on David Lynch's concrete handprints near the red carpet. Naturally, one of the photos Dane took was of our table after a nice meal in Portofino. It shows an empty plate, shot after my traditional meal of tomatoes, mozzarella, and basil. Yet again, a simple, almost pedestrian, photo, but one that shows that any Caprese salad near me would be an empty plate within minutes. It was a theme that was unique to our trip, but something that will always be a lasting memory. All trips have certain idiosyncrasies about them. The hard part is recognizing these while you're on a trip and recording them. Focus on the daily routine rather than on the big tourist sites, and you will see how your trip is full of peculiarities that define your experience.

Theme: Water

With regard to our trip, water invoked two distinct themes. There is the water of Venice and the water of Mediterranean. It's often difficult to capture, but striking in its beauty and history. Dane took two pictures of the canals in Venice that did an exceptional job of illustrating the beauty of the city. The first is a simple shot of a boat in the water. But what makes it unique is that it is shot from above and the whole boat is not in the picture, simply the bow. Over three-fourths of the picture is water. This creates a beautiful simplicity. The second shot shows a bridge over a canal. What is striking about this shot is the light coming in from under the bridge and the reflection upon the water. The beauty of water is that it's a natural mirror if you capture it correctly.

$10 Water

The second theme of water was the fact that we consumed outrageous amounts of bottled water. Dane took a picture of a bottle of water that I will never forget. We had been hiking through the hills surrounding Cannes on a 90-degree day. I had forgotten to purchase water in the morning and never had a chance throughout the day. Finally, we went to the beach in front of the Carlton Hotel to relax and watch the sunset. I was desperate for a cool, refreshing bottle of water. However, I didn't know that water was going to cost me $10! So the picture of the water has extra significance for me because it is the only $10 bottle of water I have ever heard of, and I was dumb enough to pay for it.

Theme: Maps, Plane Tickets, and Lists

Taking pictures of maps, plane tickets, and receipts provides an excellent way to frame your trip. Our photos were broken up with tickets from different legs of our journey. It starts with plane tickets, then museum tickets, then train tickets, and so on. Each shot frames the series that follows. Additionally, **finding random pieces of paper can often prove invaluable in illustrating the local culture.** They say a picture says a thousand words. Well, sometimes a picture of words can say a thousand pictures. For example, Dane and I were in a small French village getting ready for a long hike. A sudden gust of wind blew a napkin to our feet. Instead of throwing it away, Dane picked up the napkin, noticed the words on the other side, and took a picture of a very French shopping list. It was just a shopping list. But that picture becomes something more. On one level, **it shows the interconnectedness of the world.** No matter where people are, we are all making shopping lists. On another level, **it is distinctively French in its writing and content (peaches and vanilla).** Finally, the fact the peach is the only item not crossed off makes you think of a thousand scenarios as to what happened and how that shopping list landed at our feet.

I think we each had peaches for dessert that night…

Theme: Expressively Unique

One of the things Dane did to establish a theme was having me take a picture of him with his hands up in every city we visited as if to say, "Can you believe this?" At first I thought he was acting like a lunatic. I hesitantly took the picture, but would always take another when he put his hands down. Gradually, it occurred to me that Dane created a theme that took the typical "snapshot" and etched his own style into it. By the end of the trip, I was taking pictures and telling him, "Put your hands up!" Establishing your own themes can really add a new dimension to documenting your journey. Or, instead of striking a pose, you can use a prop. For example, you could bring a stuffed animal, the key-chain type, and put it in pictures all over the world. Create something that gives even greater context to your trip. At first it might seem totally crazy, but once you see the end result, it will give you a good laugh.

Memories

Everyone's journey is different, but judging from most of the pictures I see, all journeys look the same. **Avoid the big-ticket items and buy the postcard.** Looking at the pictures of our trip, I am constantly amazed at how spot-on the photos captured the feelings that we experienced during our travels. Perhaps more telling, in terms of this book, is that I also took shots on a 35mm camera. **I took 26 rolls of film. All of my pictures sit in a box in my closet.** They rarely come out to play. Dane's photos, on the other hand, play a role in my daily life. I constantly interact with them on my computer as screensavers and background, and also when I get a brief respite during the day and I want to relive those captured emotions. They take me back to sounds and smells that I miss, to a freedom that I don't get to experience too often anymore. And that was the goal, to use digital photography to capture more than an old building or notable landmark. We captured the texture of the trip—what the trip meant to us. Digital photography enables you to go beyond the ordinary.

Use it more like a paintbrush than a Polaroid and marvel at your results.

William Lamb

Chapter Review

Expressively…

Human. Your memories are a collection of stories. These stories are some of the most valued assets you will own. There is a style and an approach that is expressively your own. It is my wish that you will find them and use them over and over.

Use the techniques in this section to develop your own personalized narrative style.

When I get a brief respite during the day, I want to relive those captured emotions.

Your Story to Tell: Checklist

☐ Ask the right questions.

☐ Integrate into a daily habit.

☐ Work quickly.

☐ Author while you browse.

☐ (IIA) Immediacy, Intimacy, and Authenticity.

☐ Get closer, be flexible, and move around.

☐ Understand your structure.

☐ Remember themes when traveling.

☐ Begin now!

section 2
More Effective Images

> **In Camera**

> **Disposable Shooting**

> **Shooting a Sequence**

> **Choosing a Location**

> **Camera Settings**

> **Working Quickly**

> **Camera Placement**

> **Composition**

> **Image Acquisition**

> **On the Computer**

> **Image Editing**

"Where do you find the time to do all that?"

—colleague, just yesterday

Filename kelly_beach.jpg
Date Created 5/5/2003 07:36:17 PM
Image Format JPEG
Width 1280
Height 576
Exposure Time 1/500 sec
F-Stop 6.3
Exposure Normal
ISO Speed Ratings 100

The images you select will change based on your audience or output. Remember that the memories they evoke are contextual. Help your audience by providing this context.

More Effective Images

Effective imagery is a very personal topic. There are hundreds of resources out there to tell you how to create a technically proficient image or how to best optimize it, but very few that address how an image, sequence, or series is *effectively* communicated and experienced.

This section tries to demystify this.

You don't need the skill to capture an entire story in a single frame. The story can evolve from the fragments. A key to choosing an effective image is to select with confidence and to build on those elements and memories that mean the most to you. This will come across in its presentation.

An effective image:

> Transfers understanding (time, place, subject, and so on)

> Solicits an emotional response

> Communicates the intentions of the photographer

Great Photo!

What Are those Things That Make Us Respond to a Great Photo?

To create a more precise definition, you should talk about the experiences themselves and how you can gain control to better direct and shape (affect) those experiences. To do this, you need to locate the areas you can influence the most.

Slide Show

Digital Video

Cropping

Horizon Line   Scale

DVD

Presentation   Composition

Orientation   Position

Dynamic Media

Camera Angle

DELIVERED via...   ON COMPUTER   IN CAMERA   The "Great Photo!"

Format

Print   Format

Location

E-Mail   Image Size   Film Speed   Subject

Shutter Speed   Aperture

Web Page   Image Effects

Color Correction

Instant Message

CD-ROM

How often do you print pictures now? Perhaps save the "keepers" for a custom mailing when you know your friends and family will appreciate it.

How big is your circle of influence?

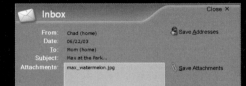

EMOTION >

A quick slideshow in a movie format gives you the ability to add further context, adding voice-over, music, or transitions.

Inbox   Close ✕

From:	Chad (home)
Date:	06/22/03
To:	Mom (home)
Subject:	Max at the Park...
Attachments:	max_watermelon.jpg

Save Addresses

Save Attachments

Mom, it was great to see you this weekend!! Thanks for the outfit. Max loves it! We can't get it off him. He squealed last night so much that we just let him sleep in it :)

See you on the 4th.
BTW: He LOVES watermelon now!

love,

Chad

If you've mastered the "attachment" to e-mail, check to see if your e-mail program will give you the ability to compose HTML e-mail, which gives you more control over the layout.

Making decisions quickly is easier with immediate feedback from the LCD panel.

In Camera

The (quick) choices you make in-camera might lend to easier editing later. I have found that photography books tend to describe the technical aspects behind making a technically proficient image. The following pages illustrate some simple techniques tailored to shooting photographs that can communicate what you intend and can give you a higher chance of creating an effective image.

"I shot over 6000 pictures last year alone."

*Chad Nelson
Designer & Daddy*

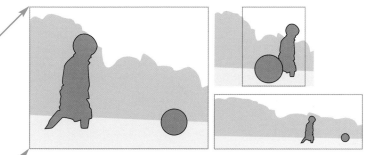

Here are three examples of the type of decisions you can make. If you can, think of each scene as a series of image compositions and decisions that you construct. Use each shot as an opportunity to grab pieces of a bigger puzzle (the untold story). As you view your images later, you'll have the opportunity to reassemble this puzzle and construct a narrative that captures how you saw the event.

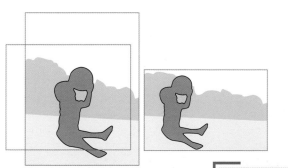

Disposable Shooting
When Cost = Free

The economics of shooting pictures has changed! It is so significant that I think it deserves its own trademark. Why should you care about it? Because it will save you a ton of money and give you a lot more freedom! You should feel okay about the opportunistic "waste" you generate.

When you start shooting with a digital camera, your mentality begins to change. You change from a scarcity mentality to an abundance mentality. You begin to realize that you can shoot hundreds of pictures on a memory card and not worry so much about wasting film or money. This was very liberating for me—and I have a photography background!

I can't say enough about what the digital camera has done for my willingness to take pictures. I found myself using it more often and more liberally. I would experiment with the settings and take advantage of the immediate feedback. If I didn't like the picture I saw, I erased it on the spot. The second thing I started to notice was that I didn't look through the viewfinder anymore. It's true! I found that when I would hold the camera out and point in the general direction, I got some amazing pictures that could only have happened by "accident."

The concept of disposable shooting has more to do with your psyche and your freedom than with the photograph itself. Disposable shooting allows you to edit the photos before they get printed. When you shoot more images, you become a better photographer. Great documentary photographers shoot an incredible number of images. To become a more effective photographer, you need to shoot a lot more. The immediate feedback the camera gives you will help drive you to make your images better. Here are a few key tips:

> **Free yourself from the viewfinder.** I find this incredibly liberating. Your images will be authentic and you'll begin to shoot differently.

> **Shoot more images in one setting.** The color and lighting will naturally create a cohesive series.

> **Shoot now, edit later.** You'll find things on your computer that you like about an image (even blurry) that you didn't see in the tiny screen on the camera. Unless you're incredibly short of space on your media card, keep the image until you can view the entire image on the computer screen.

> **Plan for Post.** You can adjust everything from color contrast and temperature to general clean-up later. In Hollywood, they call this "fixing it in Post" (post-production). If you plan on it, you can free yourself from trying to get the perfect image—you can construct it later!

I have grocery bags full of double prints that I've paid for and will never use!

The fundamental difference when shooting digital vs. film is having the ability to pay for only the images you want to keep.

TildenPark_007.JPG TildenPark_008.JPG TildenPark_009.JPG TildenPark_010.JPG TildenPark_012.JPG TildenPark_013.JPG TildenPark_043.JPG TildenPark_044.JPG

TildenPark_045.JPG TildenPark_045sm.jpg TildenPark_046.JPG TildenPark_047.JPG TildenPark_049.JPG TildenPark_054.JPG TildenPark_055.JPG TildenPark_056.JPG

TildenPark_057.JPG TildenPark_058.JPG TildenPark_059.JPG TildenPark_060.JPG TildenPark_062.JPG TildenPark_063.JPG TildenPark_074.JPG TildenPark_075.JPG

TildenPark_076.JPG TildenPark_077.JPG TildenPark_078.JPG TildenPark_079.JPG TildenPark_080.JPG TildenPark_081.JPG TildenPark_084.JPG TildenPark_089.JPG

TildenPark_093.JPG TildenPark_098.JPG TildenPark_099.JPG TildenPark_101.JPG TildenPark_102.JPG TildenPark_103.JPG TildenPark_104.JPG TildenPark_117.JPG

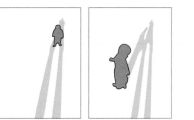

Movement and observation: **In this clever sequence based on composition, the alignment of the shadow and the position of the child were repeated quickly until the moment passed. Two specific outcomes occurred: 1) an artful composition and 2) a story of discovery by a child learning about shadows.**

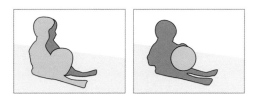

Natural light and fill flash: **This is the sequence that appears to find the elusive "keeper." When you bracket your shots by snapping multiple exposures quickly, be sure to meter on both light and dark parts of the frame for best results. Other shots used a fill flash to ensure that the face was going to be exposed despite the low and dramatic light.**

Expression hunting: **Watermelon and a two-year-old... This is a recipe for capturing the juicy expression. Notice that the fill flash is consistently used (as a failsafe) along with quick and repetitive shooting. The quick shots not only capture some great expressions, but they can now be used to illustrate a simple narrative that is all about "fun with watermelon."**

Shooting a Sequence
Watching Every Motion

When you shoot in a sequence, you have a lot of things going for you. Consistent light and a consistent subject both lend to sequence continuity. By shooting many images you can shape a narrative more effectively. I use sequences all the time when I photograph my daughter.

Try to shoot more images in one setting. Shoot a series of shots when you've chosen a context. Think about those shots in sequence. You're in an area that has consistent light, and your camera will produce an enormous range of photographs. Your chances of finding a "keeper" are better if you shoot a number of shots. Remember the disposable shooting notion! Another way to shoot a lot of images is to use a digital camcorder. Many of the new cameras have a "burst" mode on them. They are used to capture a number of images in sequence. When you shoot more images, you develop a more refined eye for viewing and editing them later.

Once you've shot a number of images, quickly review them on your camera if you can. Flip through them quickly. Order and reorder them in your head. This will play an important part when you edit and sequence them later.

Sequential images might be "poor man's video"—but they're rich in narrative.

These three images set the stage for an evening at the ball park. Each image provides specific information to answer "who, when, and where?"

WHO, WHEN, AND WHERE

When you visit a new place, put yourself in the shoes of your audience. Think about how you will visually convey your journey. Remember to take enough photographs to describe when and where the events took place, and who was there.

3. Adjust your settings to capture this light in many ways.

PACIFIC BELL PARK

HOME OF THE SAN FRANCISCO GIANTS

WILLIE MAYS GATE

PROGRAMS

4. **Return to this location later (if you can) when the light has changed. It will feel like a different place.**

2. **Walk around that area, scanning up and down.**

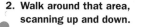

1. **Find a place where the light is really interesting.**

Choosing a Location

If you can, choose the light over the location. For a portrait, look at the overall quality of the light more than the actual location you are shooting. Near a window or door provides a beautiful source of natural light for a subject you want to get close to. If the shot is outdoors, avoid direct sunlight. A perfect spot is in the shade, but next to a bright wall or surface. The wall will reflect enough light to give a soft fill to your subject. If you've found a spot with great light, keep shooting. When you shoot multiple images, the light and color are what will make all of the shots cohesive.

SETTING A STAGE

The most effective images (and sequences) provide information about WHO, WHEN, and WHERE. This sets a foundation for a strong narrative to take place.

An Evening at the Ballpark

by Chad Nelson, Designer & Daddy

There's nothing quite like spending an evening at
the ballpark. Start with a good rivalry, add a few good
friends, and you'll find a great setting to tell a story
with photos! The challenge, however, is capturing
the essence of the event without compromising your
enjoyment of the game and evening.

When a Location Chooses You

Can't Choose a Location? Now What?!?

Try these tips:

Too light?

Too dark?

Sun is overhead?

People in the way?

> **Change film or settings.** In a night scene where there is low light, leave the shutter open longer.

> **Change your point of view.** Go low or go high to completely change the way you are viewing your location. Get closer or move farther away. The more you vary your angle and distance, the more interesting your shots will be.

> **Think in black and white.** Some camera settings will do this automatically. If you remove the color, you can concentrate more on the light. Once you've found the most interesting part(s) of your location, try moving back to color.

> **Get the pieces and fix it in "Post."** If you're planning to go on the computer anyway, shoot multiple shots of the same thing over time. Use these "pieces" to assemble your shot.

The challenge is to capture the essence of the event without compromising your enjoyment of the game.

An Evening at the Ballpark

Changing Lighting Conditions

When attending an outdoor game—
especially an evening game—expect dramatic changes in the type and quality of
light. To counter these changes, be ready
and willing to adjust camera settings as
the game progresses. In this game, for
example, the first inning was illuminated
by indirect sunlight. By centering the camera on the interior of the stadium, the
camera's AUTO mode was able to accommodate for the shaded stadium interior.
During later innings, I switched to Manual
mode to allow for the artificial stadium
lights. In this mode, I was able to control
the aperture and white-balance to best
match natural light (see below).

**You can use your image editing software (here it's
Adobe Photoshop Elements File Browser) to view
specific information about your camera's settings.
I've used this information to learn about which settings produce the most desirable outcomes. You
can then use these for future reference.**

Filename	$_22.JPG
Date Created	7/2/2003 05:35:15 AM
Date Modified	4/23/2002 12:31:22 PM
Image Format	JPEG
Width	1280
Height	960
Color Mode	RGB
File Size	550K
Image Description	
Make	SONY
Model	CYBERSHOT
Orientation	Normal
X Resolution	72.0
Y Resolution	72.0
Resolution Unit	Inches
Date Time	2002:04:23 19:31:23
yCbCr Positioning	Cosited
Exposure Time	1/125 sec
F-Stop	2.8
Exposure Program	Normal program
ISO Speed Ratings	100
ExifVersion	0210
Date Time Original	2002:04:23 19:31:23
Date Time Digitized	2002:04:23 19:31:23
Components Configuration	Unknown
Compressed Bits Per Pixel	2.0
Exposure Bias Value	0.0
Max Aperture Value	2.0
Metering Mode	Center Weighted Average
Light Source	Tungsten
Flash	Did not fire.
Focal Length	21.0 mm
FlashPix Version	0100
EXIF Color Space	sRGB
Pixel X Dimension	1280
Pixel Y Dimension	960
File Source	DSC
Scene Type	Direct Photographed Image

Change Your Film and Settings

As the light changes, so should your settings. Whether you change the settings or your camera, you should know what's happening.

This is a simple example of two shots taken with different lighting settings. The top one was taken with the "Daylight" setting. The one on the bottom was taken with the "Tungsten" setting (also called Indoor on many cameras).

> **Outdoors/Daylight:** Most cameras handle daylight acceptably in AUTO mode. One tip, however, is to consider using a flash when the sun is too bright (see "Effective Flash" on page 92).

> **Outdoors/Dusk:** When the light starts to fade, experiment with Manual mode rather than immediately turning on the flash. Most of the basic digital cameras have a Dusk/Sunset mode... so be willing to experiment with those modes first.

> **Indoors:** Fluorescent, Tungsten, Halogen... unless you plan to become an expert on artificial lighting, just think of these as indoor lights. Most cameras have an Indoor mode that will be acceptable with most types of lights. If you still find your colors slightly off, experiment with either AUTO or Outdoor mode. You might be surprised when one of those works!

> **Mixed Light:** I find there are many occasions when the lighting is mixed with indoor illumination and sunlight streaming in through a window. In these situations, I set the camera to what I feel is the dominant light source. If I'm still uncertain, I can experiment with all the settings and see instant results! That's the beauty of digital.

Most people think of camera settings as either right or wrong—which can become intimidating. Rather, think of the settings on your camera in terms of better or worse.

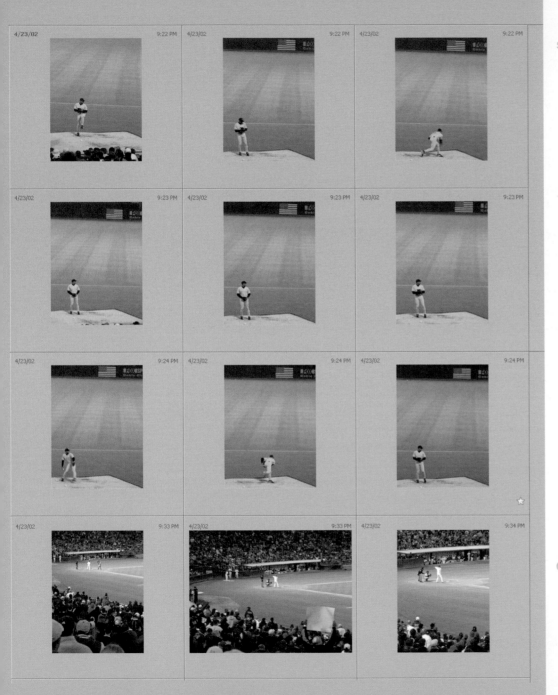

Section 3, row 4, seat 7

An Evening at the Ballpark

Change Your Point of View

How do you capture the spectacle, the excitement, or the meaning of a baseball game? A tough task indeed—especially when you're only one person with one camera. My strategy for getting around this is simple—move around! Capturing an event is about coverage; covering the core action and the side movements, as well as the overall surroundings. In this game, I started with wide shots of the field, the scoreboard, and the crowd. Then I began to focus on individual moments. At one point, I decided to take a longer route back to my seat. As I did, I found a relief pitcher warming up on the sidelines. No big deal. But then I noticed the American flag directly behind him. Taking the longer route produced an unexpected shot, and one that, arguably, captured the essence of baseball better than any other I took that night.

Section 17, row 12, seat 4

Section 19, row 24, seat 1

Change Your Point of View

Watch a sporting event, a movie, or even a simple talk show and you'll notice they have multiple angles from multiple vantage points. This creates more interest and makes the viewer more immersed in the scene, event, or action. Applying some of these simple tricks can separate the boring photo album or home video from something that is truly entertaining and engaging!

> **Think high. Think low. Think all-around!** If you wanted to photograph, for example, your child's first-grade class-room…how would you capture it? Don't stop after you snap a wide shot of the room! Take a shot from the perspective of the child's desk. Try another from behind the teacher's desk. Soon you'll find yourself bouncing around the room capturing shots!

> **Get close…and then closer!** Most people have a tendency to capture the wide shot, but never take a moment to capture the details. Think about the smaller things (shells on the beach) or the singular thing (a single flower in the room) when framing some of your shots. This will add a nice balance and diversity to your photo series.

> **If you have the time—use it!** Some shots are easy to capture. Others require a bit more effort. But if you find yourself imagining the perfect shot from a location other than where you are…if you have the time—go for it!

> **And one of my favorite tips:** When you enter a scene or location, take a shot of the first thing you see and the last thing you notice before you leave. This will give you some nice "bookends" for a photo series.

Move around! Capturing an event is about coverage: covering the core action and the side movements, as well as the overall surroundings.

An Evening at the Ballpark

Think in Black and White

The game had come to a close, and the crowd quickly filed out of the stadium. I decided to look over the stadium to capture a few final images. What struck me were differences between a stadium filled and one nearly empty. I switched my camera into Black and White mode to better focus on this stark contrast. What I found: the environment, once saturated with motion and color, had transformed into a solemn world of black and gray.

A great trick in Adobe Photoshop Elements is to click on one of the channels (Red, Green, or Blue) and see which channel gives you the best image. If you select all (CTRL A) and copy/paste into a new document, you now have a rich black and white photo.

The environment, once saturated with motion and color, had transformed into a solemn world of black and gray.

Many cameras have a Sepia mode on them. This can offer a fresh perspective to your images, especially when you show them off later. It can create a warm point of emphasis.

Think in Black and White

Shoot in Black and White mode whenever possible. It forces you to see (and think) differently about your composition. You'll start to see the world in contrast and gray values. If your camcorder or digital camera has a

Black and White mode, use it. Removing color is sometimes the most effective way to remove additional complexity. It's also a great way to remove a color temperature that might be distracting.

An Evening at the Ballpark

Get the Pieces, and Fix it in "Post"

How do you get a picture of the yourself holding up a
"SELLOUT" sign in front of a capacity crowd the very
moment a player steps up to bat for the first time as an
opposing player? The answer is…you don't. To capture
that moment in a single photograph requires too much
coordination, planning, and luck. However, this is one of
the great benefits of digital imaging. Using a program
like Adobe Photoshop Elements or Microsoft Picture It!
Digital Image Pro, it's possible to combine several shots
together to create a singular moment. So how did I get
this shot? I took one shot for the background, one with
the player in position, and a final shot with me holding
the sign (at the end of the game so I wouldn't disturb
anyone).

**Here is a great example of how sitting in one place (like at a baseball
game) will give you a multitude of shot elements to use and play with
later. Notice that even the batter can be used to compose the final shot.**

Get the Pieces, and Fix it in "Post"

> **Consistent lighting:** If you plan to compose a shot in color, be sure that you can color-match the light temperature of your different shots. Shoot quickly and be sure to keep a steady camera.

> **Consistent settings:** This will help you unify the image later. I have seen variable shutter speeds that allow you to use motion blur effectively, but don't vary your color settings or light temperature.

> **Think in layers:** Give yourself the ability to think in three dimensions. Try to separate the image into distinct background, middle ground, and foreground elements.

The finished composite image is better than a keeper; it's perfect.

Camera Settings

Your camera's spec sheet is pretty impressive, but keeping all those features straight can quickly become overwhelming. Start simple. I like to think of the most important settings choice as manual or automatic. Plus, I almost always turn off the flash, regardless—but that's just me.

Point-and-click modes put the camera in control. You should try to take back some of this control by adjusting your ISO settings.

1 The first thing I do when I turn my camera on is **turn off the flash**.

2 The second thing I do is decide if I'm going to shoot in automatic or manual.

3 The third thing I do is I forget about the viewfinder. I use the LCD whenever I can. This gives me a certain freedom when shooting and observing events develop.

4 Shoot! I start shooting. When I'm done, I shoot some more.

Choosing ISO and Camera Settings

With traditional film cameras, you need to weigh a lot of technical considerations when choosing film, but your main concern is how sensitive that film is to the light. With digital cameras, your main concern is how sensitive your camera is responding to the lighting condition in the scene. Digital cameras replicate film sensitivity through an electronic sensor that captures and interprets light conditions pixel-by-pixel. It's not necessary to choose your "film" with a digital camera; however, you'll want to test the range of the camera setting by exploring the full range of its aperture and shutter speeds based on your ISO setting. Most digital cameras allow you to set the sensitivity to replicate film conditions. With ISO settings, the higher the number, the more sensitive your camera will be to light. An ISO setting of 400 will allow you to shoot in lower light than a setting of 50 would.

If you have a digital camera, it's helpful to think as if there is film in the camera, only because you'll think then about how you want to shoot. Point-and-click puts the camera in control. You should try to take back some of this control. When you think about light sensitivity, it forces you to think about the light, and then you're focusing on the right things.

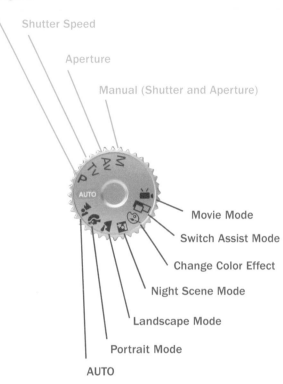

Program

Shutter Speed

Aperture

Manual (Shutter and Aperture)

Movie Mode

Switch Assist Mode

Change Color Effect

Night Scene Mode

Landscape Mode

Portrait Mode

AUTO

The specific modes or icons of your camera might be a little different, but the basic principles are the same. This camera is a Canon G2.

MANUAL

Selecting Specific Effects

Most cameras will allow you to isolate one or all of the settings listed above in some type of manual mode, but fundamentally you'll find that the most significant changes will occur with the relationship between shutter speed and aperture (iris). These two work closely together to determine the exposure and focal length (see the diagram on page 95). The best way to learn is to work in manual and try it out (a lot).

AUTOMATIC

Letting the Camera Select Settings

Automatic covers a lot: auto focus, auto aperture, auto shutter speed, and auto flash. If you are in an automatic mode, take advantage of what is "automatic" about it. Shooting in automatic helps you think about things outside the camera rather than how the image is captured in-camera. You can generally do the following better when shooting in automatic:

> **Shoot faster.** Snap the shutter, not the settings.

> **Hand-hold.** Lose the formal tripod.

> **Forget the viewfinder.** See the bigger picture.

> **Think.** Consider the location, light, angle, composition, presentation, story, and so on.

Resource: Digital Camera Resource (www.dcresource.com) is a great online site to compare and contrast the latest in digital camera models and their features.

1 Turn Off the Flash! Your camera is really versatile. It will do what it needs to get the light. The only thing you might get is motion blur. Stick with it.

2 Survey the Scene. Spot meter the areas where your subject may move throughout the space. In this example, the light changed quite a bit, but the settings exposure on the face seemed to remain about the same.

3 Skin Tone. Find it and follow it. This will give you the softness and the flexibility you'll need to crop and edit later.

4 Stay with Them... You'll find that you will eventually capture the essense of your subjects if you just stay with them. Missed opportunities happen too frequently when we stop shooting.

Great Portraits—Every Time
Spot Metering

I learned a great trick when shooting portraits using the in-camera light meter. If you're shooting manually, you can walk right up to your subject (as close as three inches) and meter the darker side of the face. Then step back and compose your shot. You'll notice that your meter rating will either be above or below your mark. Don't change it! You've metered correctly for the skin tones in the the face, so it will be in the correct exposure. Skin tone is the most important exposure when doing a simple portrait. I also can get great results when I shoot in automatic by spot metering. On my camera, this is when I press the shutter button down halfway. It will correctly meter whatever is inside the square. You can use this trick on just about anything within the composition for which you want a correct exposure.

Don't do this! This was my first shot. I immediately turned the flash off. Notice that the camera automatically looks for light and fires the flash when it needs additional light. By turning off the flash and using the spot meter, I just target the areas I want in the correct exposure.

My "keeper" happened once I began a simple game of "peek-a-boo" with my daughter. My exposure was set, which gave me the freedom to get just enough of my daughter's attention span to snap a couple shots of her peeking over the table.

Three Minutes with My Daughter

When my daughter Chloe began walking, I found that most of my frustration in capturing a good image of her happened because I was expecting that she would hold still long enough for me to take her picture. Duh! I decided I would use short, active shooting sequences where I would follow her around and walk alongside of her. I would move the camera, position it low, high—literally shooting from the hip. I tried to focus on the "essence" of her mobility and tell short little stories about simple things (new shoes, red hat, or the toy she was playing with). By shooting quickly and in short bursts, I could feel confident that I was capturing some very real behavior and something that authentically captured what she was doing. By following her, I gave myself time to observe her. After three minutes if I was able to get a single image I liked, I called it a success.

When three minutes were up, I took a breather.

She kept going...

Here are four key things to think about when working quickly:

> **Anticipate movement.** View the characters and those things that are the most likely to change. This may be subjects or it may be the light. If you can anticipate this change, you can make better choices on setting up the shot, exposure, and angle.

> **Bracket your shots.** Use multiple types of exposure settings. As you shoot quickly, vary your settings to get a range of shots.

> **Change your angle often.** Changing your settings can be disruptive and time-consuming, but in most cases, you can change your angle very quickly.

> **Keep the motion blur; it's cool.** Use this natural effect to your advantage. This naturally communicates motion and immediacy and gives a sense of motion, particularly when presented in sequence.

Start

30 sec.

Working Quickly

This takes getting used to. Know your surroundings and what you're trying to achieve in the image. People are hard. Babies and kids are the toughest. Low-light sun shots are also difficult (when working with quickly changing light conditions).

Working quickly is thinking about the photograph before it starts to happen.

Again, watch the light. People and light move quickly. If you have a choice, try to wrestle with the light more than with the person. This has a lot to do with moving quickly around your subject and letting your subject move naturally through the space and the light. If your subject is a child, you have to move around a lot. You're in charge of composition and the exposure. Work quickly, but try not to control too many things at once.

**DON'T WORRY—
MOTION BLUR
IS COOL**

Try tracking your camera with fast moving subjects. You want to make sure you have clarity on those parts of the image that you care about most.

Shooting quickly usually means setting your camera for faster shutter speeds to "stop" the action. Try not to worry too much about this. Fast action and movement usually creates a natural motion blur in the image. One way to do this is to track the head movement of your subject with the camera. This is difficult to do, but it's effective when it works. What you get is a still head with a motion blur in the background.

2 min.

3 min.

Widbey Island Ferry

The panorama can be a great technique to show the breadth of a view. Some cameras have panorama modes that allow you to compose entire sequences, enabling you to align the horizon line in camera.

Horizon Line

San Francisco Bay

MORE INTERESTING CITYSCAPES

One of the most basic decisions you can make when shooting a landscape or cityscape is choosing where your horizon line will be placed.

Camera Placement and Horizon Lines
Land and Cityscapes

Good photographs can become great photographs if you simply think about camera placement. One way to illustrate this is in landscape photography. The tendency is to put the horizon right in the center of the frame. If you move the camera up or down, the horizon line creates two entirely different and compelling images. You can do the same thing when shooting people. Move the camera up and down, side to side. Composition and placement will result in some extraordinary pictures. In many situations, you are much more agile than your subjects. Feel comfortable about moving quickly to test out different camera placements.

05/09/03

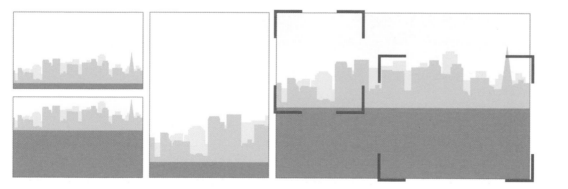

Horizon lines will contribute greatly to your composition and the interest of your photograph. These decisions are valuable both in-camera and on your computer if you plan to crop. If you have resolution to spare, a balanced shot will give you multiple cropping options.

REMEMBER:

Before you snap the shot, move your horizon line to the upper or lower third of the frame. More interesting shots will result.

Horizon Line

A great way to force a strong horizon line is to set your camera on the floor. Not only is this helpful when you're alone (to set the timer), but it will give you a perspective you're not used to.

Camera Placement and Horizon Lines
People and Places

Not every picture you take of a person or place will have an obvious horizon line, but you will be able to think about it the same way as you do with cityscapes or landscapes. A simple, conscious decision to move the "dominant" horizontal line into the upper or lower third of the frame is a powerful tool for you to compose your shots. Give yourself a bunch of options by shooting the same image low, middle, and high. Give yourself the flexibility to choose later which shot works better for you.

COMPOSITION

Your primary focus will be on your subject. The horizon line will become a valuable composition element that will bring strength and focus to your image.

The camera tilt is a simple but effective way to compose your portraits to give you a lot of flexibility when editing later.

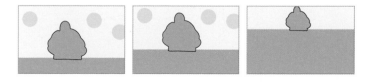

Photography is merely "painting"... ...with light.

Light: Natural and Artificial

Some professionals have spent their entire career studying the qualities of light. Like much of the history of photography, there is certainly a science in studying it. The more you know about how light behaves on surfaces, the better off you'll be in creating effective images.

This means turn off the flash!

A flash is used as an overkill factor to guarantee that your pictures will "come out." It usually floods the subject with front light. When you start to look at light, you start to see the world differently.

When you start documenting things as they are, you'll experience all kinds of lighting conditions.

I recommend using natural light whenever possible.

I think there is no more emphatic statement I could make other than to look at light as a fundamental quest to capture wonderful images.

Lighting Situations
by Don Barnett, Designer, Photographer, & Father

(1) Sunlight

Direct sunlight is the most harsh when directly overhead, creating very dark shadows with a lot of contrast. See if you can get your subjects out of the direct sunlight and find some way to diffuse the light. For example:

> **Shoot when cloud cover or haze is present.** This tends to diffuse the light and soften the harshness of direct sunlight.

> **Use reflective light.** The light found in shadows is a trick professional photographers use all the time. Try a nearby concrete wall or a windshield shade.

(2) Reflected Light

This is the ideal light. In the shade on a bright day, the light is wonderfully diffused. Objects beyond your subject are in the background and in full sun will get overexposed when you meter for the objects in the shade.

(3) Incandescent Light

Indoor light bulbs tend to be warm in color. The light can be very desirable if properly exposed. If a digital camera is set for outdoor sunlight, the image can be yellow-orange. Check your camera and the color temperature settings. Be sure to set the color balance for sun or indoor lights separately, or outdoor shots can look blue and indoor shots can look orange. Sometimes this effect can be used to your advantage. In either circumstance, using a weak fill flash can succeed in balancing out the color temperature.

(4) Moonlight/Lowlight

Minimal light calls for fast film (ASA speeds of 400 up) and long exposure times. Portraits are difficult, but landscapes are easily accomplished with a tripod or some way to stabilize the camera. Moonlight photos tend to be monochromatic unless very long exposures are used, which can result in unusual and exaggerated color effects.

(5) Candlelight and Firelight

Wonderfully sensitive and soft portraits can be shot by candlelight or firelight. Your subject needs to remain fairly still due to low light, and these shots require longer exposure times. Constantly moving sources of light (such as a camp fire) cause very soft edges, but dark and dramatic shadows.

1

2

3

4

5

The Cycles of Light

Direct light creates a hard-edged shadow with a variety of lengths and directions. Reflected light creates softer shadows.

Effective Flash

by Damon Nelson, Designer, Photographer, & Uncle

The electronic flash is an excellent tool to provide adequate lighting on your subject regardless of the natural light you have available. With either a built-in flash or an external flash unit, you give yourself the flexibility to shoot great pictures in nearly any given situation.

Here are some basics to remember:

> **A flash has a limited range.** It might seem that the light produced by your flash is very powerful (and it is); however, the light decreases very rapidly as it travels. While the flash might brightly light an object in the foreground, objects in the background might remain in shadows. Increasing the power of your flash to compensate will only blow out the detail on the foreground object. Instead, try to position your subjects at a similar distance to the camera so that the flash can light them evenly. If you are shooting in low light and you are getting black backgrounds, make sure your subjects are in front of a background that is relatively close like a wall or other surface.

> **You can always use a flash.** If you are taking your camera out on a sunny day, don't leave the flash behind. It might seem like an odd idea, but a flash can be extremely useful to fill in harsh shadows created by daylight and will allow you to position your subjects with more versatility. Try positioning someone with the sun off to one side so that the sun creates strong shadows across the face. Then experiment with your flash to see if you can fill in the shadows while maintaining detail. Check your flash settings to see if it has a "fill flash" mode—this helps fill in shadows without overpowering your subject in daylight.

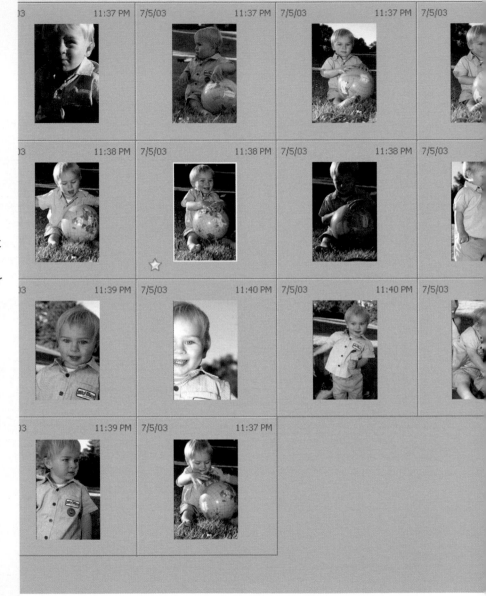

Fill **Flash**

If photography is painting with light, using a flash is like giving you a brush.

Professional photographers use strobes (varieties of a flash) all the time to manipulate their settings and simulate natural light, even in impossible situations. Most consumer cameras use a flash that is mounted onto the camera, which can be limiting. As I mentioned before, I recommend that you turn this flash off whenever possible. If you can, find a way to connect a flash to your camera using an extension cord. Use one hand to hold the camera, and the other to hold and point the flash from different angles. This way, you can bounce the light off other objects and get results that you can't get with a mounted flash.

A fill flash can fill in the shadows while maintaining detail.

An effective flash is a fill flash, a setting designed not to bleach out your subject. A flash that goes off from the side or overhead will give a more natural look and better depth. The most important aspect of a fill flash is that it bounces off another object to create reflected light. Try bouncing it off a white ceiling or a side wall to get a great reflected light.

	Left	Right
Y Resolution	72.0	72.0
Resolution Unit	Inches	Inches
Date Time	2001:10:26 18:11:09	2001:10:26 18:32:08
yCbCr Positioning	Cosited	Cosited
Exposure Time	1/100 sec	1/5 sec
F–Stop	2.1	2.1
Exposure Program	Shutter priority	Shutter priority
ISO Speed Ratings	100	100
ExifVersion	0210	0210
Date Time Original	2001:10:26 18:11:09	2001:10:26 18:32:08

Color: **Painting with Light**

Color is related to light, yet the way a camera interprets color is a science and an art in itself. It's also really fun to play with. Digital image editing programs allow color alterations to be viewed almost instantly.

Because color relates to image capture in-camera, it's important that you understand the nuances in the language of color and what it can communicate.

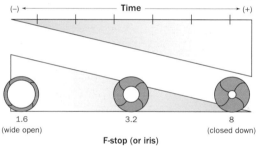

TIME EXPOSURE

Time exposure is like soaking an image with light. The longer you leave the shutter open, the more "saturated" with light your image will become until it is completely white.

Whatever your preference, be sure that your camera interprets color to your desired preference when you need this. Accurate color in-camera is certainly a personal preference. I've seen professional photographers shoot Russian-made cameras built in the 1960s simply because they capture and interpret the light and color a little differently.

The same is true with digital cameras. You'll notice differences from brand to brand on how cameras capture and interpret color. Just about all of the good photography reviews allow you to compare and contrast images taken by different cameras under similar conditions.

In this example, the cityscape of San Francisco shows the difference between a 1/100 second exposure vs. a 1/5 second exposure. Setting a camera on a ledge or table will assist you in creating such images.

Near Infrared

by Eric Cheng, Photographer, & Computer Scientist

In Camera

Near-infrared photography has long been practiced in both practical and artistic photographic endeavors. In the near-infrared spectrum, healthy foliage takes on a brilliant whiteness and bright blue skies darken to a pitch black. The resulting images often have a ghost-like, ethereal quality to them.

To see if your digital camera is capable of recording near-infrared images, point the front of any infrared remote control at your camera and press one of its buttons. If you can see a light flashing on your digital camera's LCD screen, your camera can take near-infrared photographs! Next, you will need to acquire a filter that blocks out all visible light (commonly called a "hot-mirror" filter). The specific filter you need will vary according to your camera model, but common filters include the R72, #88a, #89b, and #87 filters, which are available at many local and online camera stores. You can also make your own filter by using frames of developed-but-unexposed film and placing them in front of your camera's lens. Because unmodified digital cameras aren't very sensitive to near-infrared light, shutter speeds will be long; use a tripod to get sharp shots.

For more information on digital infrared photography, point your browser to: **http://echeng.com/photo/infrared/**

In Computer

Infrared-like effects and other interesting black and white looks can be accomplished by separating the individual color channels of a given image. Looking at the red, green, or blue channel individually (by using the channels palette in an image editor such as Adobe Photoshop) can often produce vastly different looks in the black and white version of an image. For even more flexibility, you can use a channel mixer to combine individual channels into a single black and white image to get the look that you want. (In Adobe Photoshop, go to Image > Adjustments > Channel Mixer and make sure "Monochrome" is checked.) Incidentally, famous nature photographers such as Ansel Adams used red filters to make their black and white images look dramatic. You can do the same thing by favoring the red channel in your channel-mixing experiments.

In this example, a #82 filter is used to extract the values needed for the infrared.

The original color image is brought into Adobe Photoshop, where a single channel is isolated, then copied into a new document for further editing and levels adjustment.

Scale and **Contrast**

Big or small aren't usually that interesting by themselves, but placed next to each other they are very interesting. This creates contrast. Getting closer to your subject produces more intimate images. This is true for still-life images and portraits. The very premise of the word "scale" suggests contrast, and when you think about building an effective image or series of images, keep this in mind. On the other end of the spectrum, you can show a sense of scale when your location is especially large compared to your subject.

Using scale and contrast can give you powerful juxtapositions. Use close-up shots for intimacy and texture. Use distance shots to establish location or scale.

Use Multiple Images: Scale and contrast can be very powerful tools for multiple images. Use them to frame a context or narrative when you share your images. The juxtaposition between the images will be more powerful than what you can do with a single image.

June 16, 2003

"She had watched us hold the new baby, and she wanted to do the same. There is a softness and tenderness in her that I haven't seen expressed that way."

Here are some things to keep in mind when shooting and editing using scale and contrast:

① **Eyes and Hands:** Appear intimate and narrative in nature.

② **Selective Focus:** Creates a dynamic and natural emphasis.

③ **Composition:** Includes basic shapes, such as triangles, and abstracts.

④ **Juxtaposition:** Opposites are naturally interesting: color with black and white, small vs. big, smooth vs. rough, tall vs. short, and so on.

⑤ **Rhythm and Cadence:** Scale and contrast create a natural variation when images appear in a sequence or in succession.

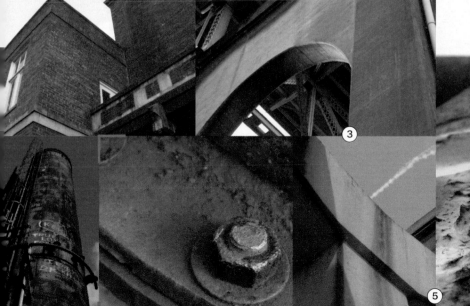

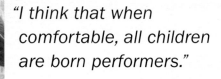

"*I think that when comfortable, all children are born performers.*"

Capturing Children

by Emily Palmgren, Former Stock Broker, Photographer, & Mommy

Children are really fun to photograph. When left to be themselves, uncoached, they never fail to be brilliantly beautiful. There is an innocence and sweetness that children have—a freshness, I guess you might say, that I try to portray. When you are the parent of a child, you want to savor and capture moments—to stop the clock, just for a second so that you can hold onto an expression or gesture—the essence of what makes your child unique.

No two kids are alike. An energetic child will move differently around you than a quiet child. I try to capture this by shooting from different angles and by using different lens lengths and shutter speeds. Usually it is the child who will define the tone and feeling of how we interact. By taking the child's lead, you will get a truer portrayal of who he or she is.

It is important to be aware of your subject's comfort level. Some kids strike a pose right off the bat. Others may be more reserved. I try to connect with each one differently and make sure each feels safe and important. I usually invite quieter children to help me set up or even let them take some pictures of me or other family members. I spend time with the parent talking, and not paying any attention to the goal (the "perfect" shot). And, if all else fails, we reschedule. Most of the time, though, when my subjects realize they are free and safe, their personalities start to come out and they are really fun to catch on film.

I find that the best pictures are the ones that are not coached by myself or by the parents. Sometimes I will make silly conversation asking them their favorite candy or cartoon character or asking them if they can see themselves in the lenses. But rarely do I say, "Smile and look at the camera."

When you are trying to tell a story through pictures you have to be willing to shoot a lot of film (images). I learned this when I bought my digital point-and-shoot camera. I would shoot 50 shots at a park play date, come home, edit out the 5–10 I liked, and discard the rest. A digital camera can be a great, inexpensive learning tool in this way. Although my professional work is done on film, I often use a digital camera to take a couple of test shots for light.

Composition Elements
by Don Barnett, Designer & Father

Here is a list of some basic composition principles to keep in mind when you shoot and edit your images:

> **Lines and Direction:** Lines in an image have a real impact to the end result of a composition.
>
> Horizontal and vertical lines add stability (for example, horizons or architecture). Diagonal lines ② add a dynamic element. Lines can lead the eye to a key area in the photograph. The direction a person is looking (the line of sight) can also effect the composition. A person on the right side of a photo looking back toward the center of the photo can help keep the composition balanced.
>
> Conversely, a person looking off the frame ① should be balanced with another strong element in the composition. Without that balance, the eye is led off the edge, and this can cause a sense of imbalance. You can, however use imbalance to your advantage when you put images into a narrative sequence to encourage direction and flow.

> **Motion and Direction:** Many effective images contribute to moving the eye in a strong direction through the image. These compositions keep the movement intentional and directed, yet keep the eye moving through the image. ① When a subject is in motion, it will lead the viewer's eye. Our brain anticipates where the subject is moving and the eye will be drawn ahead of the motion. Take this into consideration when balancing a composition. ②

> **Depth of Field:** Focus can be used as a strong compositional element. ③ A short depth of field is when only a small amount of depth in a scene is in focus. It is helpful to isolate the subjects you want to stand out. If the background around a subject you want to shoot is soft and out of focus, there is much more emphasis on the subject and less cluttering detail that can distract. This is done by opening the aperture or using lower numbered f-stops.
>
> You can also fake depth of field by digitally manipulating the image. (See "On Your Computer," on page 107.)

> **Focal Point:** A well-articulated focal point will give the eye a natural starting point. ③ It's like the beginning of the story for that specific image. Use this to your advantage and use lines, direction, motion, and depth of field to create and control your focal point.
>
> The simpler the image is, the more direct the visual impact. Concentrate on simple shapes and converging lines for impact. Sometimes a photo with too many elements can be confusing. A great way to remove complexity is to get closer. Remember that a photograph is a flat plane in which all that your eye sees in the real world gets compressed together. There might be too much information to sort out on the flat plane of a photograph.

> **Value:** Shooting black and white can help a photographer to see form and contrasts better. ④ This will directly improve color photography. Look for areas of dark and light. Where the darkest dark meets the lightest light is the area which will attract the most attention contrast wise. Use it to your advantage compositionally. If shooting a silouhette, put the contrast behind the area on the subject you want to emphasize. Likewise, downplay contrast where it is needed least. If background is not important to the photo composition, it would suit the photograph to have little change in contrast in the background.

Composition

I like to think of an image's composition as telling a miniature story. This "story" needs to be read. It's your job to compose and crop the image to better guide the eye through this story. You can break up this story by looking at its structure. You can create a visual hierarchy that presents the viewer with a natural "read" through the image. This read is usually broken into three parts. There are a number of tricks you can use in composing your images to help influence a more effective read.

I think of every composition as an opportunity to tell a mini-story.

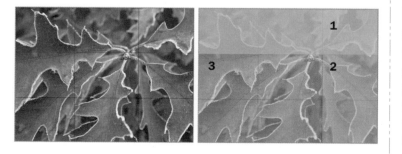

RULE OF THIRDS

Studies have shown that the human eye goes naturally to a point two thirds up the page. This composition might not have been as interesting with the convergence of the leaves in the center.

1 When your computer first detects your camera or media, it will give you an opportunity to choose what you'd like to do with it. With Microsoft Digital Library 9 installed, you get additional choices to import and edit.

MEDIA (F:)

Windows can perform the same action each time you insert a disk or connect a device with this kind of file:

Pictures

What do you want Windows to do?

- Edit pictures
  using Adobe Photoshop Elements
- Import pictures to my computer
  using Microsoft Digital Image import wizard
- Open and edit the pictures
  using Microsoft Picture It! Express 7.0
- Open folder to view files
  using Windows Explorer
- Take no action

☐ Always do the selected action.

[OK] [Cancel]

Import Pictures Wizard

Welcome to the Import Pictures Wizard

Import your pictures and video clips from your camera or other storage device into Digital Image Library.

How would you like to import your pictures and video clips?

- ● Copy them to my computer or network. The pictures will be cataloged in Digital Image Library automatically.
- ○ Catalog them in Digital Image Library, but leave them in their current location.

The catalog-only option is available for compatible devices, such as photo CDs, DVDs, or other mass storage media.

To continue, click Next.

Help

[< Back] [Next >] [Cancel]

2 When working with multiple image/media types, figure out where you'd like to keep most of your media. In most cases, you will copy the media to your hard drive to create more room on your media card inside your camera.

3 Selecting your media is the next step. The wizard will assume that you want to copy all of the media. Holding down the CTRL key while selecting thumbnails will allow you to deselect those that you don't want to transfer.

Import Pictures Wizard

Pictures and Video Clips to Copy
Select the pictures you want to copy. All pictures are selected by default. To select individual files, click Clear All, and then press CTRL as you click each file.

IMG_4025   IMG_4027   IMG_4039

IMG_4040   IMG_4044   IMG_4045

[Clear All] [Select All]

23 picture(s) selected of 23

[< Back] [Next >] [Cancel]

Import Pictures Wizard

Picture Name and Destination
Choose a group name, folder-naming style, and destination.

1. Type a name for this group of pictures:

   Month_date

   ☑ Rename pictures using this group name. For example: Holiday 001, Holiday 002.

2. From the drop-down list, click a naming style for the new folder. If you want to save to a destination other than My Pictures, click Browse.

   My Pictures\Month_date   [Browse...]

☐ Delete pictures from my device after copying them

Help

[< Back] [Next >] [Cancel]

4 Selecting your copy destination gives you a perceptual location for your media. I usually date my folders according to when I took the photos. For more information on organizing your photos, see Section 3.

Image Acquisition
What You Get

Transferring your media from a device to the computer is certainly easier than it has been in the past. The two main things you have to think about are:

> **Location:** Where do you want them copied? You'll have to retrieve them later.

> **Naming/Keywords:** What do you want to name them? You'll have to understand the names later.

Did you know… your Compact Flash or (other) media card can also be used to transfer images back onto it? All you need is a media card reader. This gives you flexibility to treat the card like an external storage disk. You can then bring this card to a photo developer to get the images printed.

When you acquire an image (today), you get a lot more than just the image. Your camera may capture a lot of information about the image when it was taken. The information associated with the image is like a profile of itself. The acquisition software you use will increasingly take advantage of this extra information (automatically) to help you organize and edit your imagery.

<date> <time>

<date>
<time>
<camera settings>
<format>
<location>
<who>
<what>
<keyword 1>
<keyword 2>
<etc...>

The images that need fixing might already be grouped together because the camera said they were "underexposed" when they were taken. Likewise, images of people might be grouped separately from landscape shots. Facial recognition might auto detect and suggest a cropping modification.

SMARTER ACQUISITION

The good news is that software is getting increasingly smarter. It will remember the location and automate the naming. The location of your images on your hard drive will become increasingly less important as query-driven interfaces will allow you to auto-sort your media by groups of media that are categorized. For more information, see "Annotation" on page 130 in Section 3.

105

IMG_4024

When the images are on your computer, you'll be barraged with browsing choices and editing choices. For the sake of your time (and sanity), you'll need to know what to look for when the editing process begins.

IMG_4032

IMG_4040

On Your Computer

I've learned some simple, yet incredible, ways to make images more effective. All those problem shots need is a little rescuing.

IMG_4048

THE UNLIKELY HERO

Some of my most interesting images in the end were those that I rescued and then became "keepers". Don't discard an image if it doesn't strike you right away. It might grab you later. Give some of those shots a chance to be heroes.

IMG_4056

IMG_4064

You might find yourself rescuing your images after you transfer them to your computer.

turn out great...

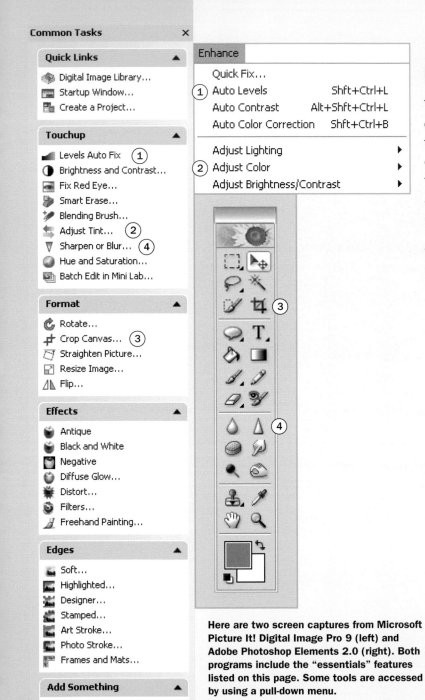

Here are two screen captures from Microsoft Picture It! Digital Image Pro 9 (left) and Adobe Photoshop Elements 2.0 (right). Both programs include the "essentials" features listed on this page. Some tools are accessed by using a pull-down menu.

Image Editing

There are dozens of software programs that will allow you to crop, color-correct, colorize, and manipulate your photos. The best programs are those that meet your budget and your needs. Often, too much choice can bog down the process and take too much time. I suggest keep it simple and look for something with a "batch" processing function for doing repetitive tasks automatically. I use about 1/20th of the image editing tools available to me. Here are some key tools to use and master:

THE BASICS

(1) **Levels (Brightness/Contrast):** Ability to lighten or darken various tonal ranges within a photo.

(2) **Color Balance:** Ability to shift color across various tonal ranges within a photo. Be sure the tool gives you the ability to shift color in the lights, mid-tones, and darks independently.

(3) **Crop:** One of the most basic tools, but great when used well.

(4) **Sharpen:** When images get resized, they soften up. You'll need to sharpen them.

NOW YOU'RE TALKING

> **Selection:** Ability to isolate and manipulate a part of an image with increasing control. Might include a feathered edge.

> **Layers:** Ability to manipulate a 2D image and various parts of an image independently from each other.

> **Cloning:** Ability to copy one part of an image and transfer (clone) it to another part of the image. This is also called a "transfer" brush, and the technique is a great way to erase or extend specific parts of an image.

original

① brightness/contrast

② color balance

③ crop

AUTOMATION

Many software packages allow you to record a series of tasks and then play them back on an image-by-image basis. To take it one step further, they even allow you to execute a similar set of functions on an entire folder of images, keeping your originals for backup. I like to call this "Shake and Bake" for images. For more information, see Section 3.

By erasing the blur on the top layer, I can literally "paint"
the image into focus, giving me ultimate control over
directing the eye through the composition.

Selective Focus
Erase the Blur

Selective focus is a natural optical technique used by photographers to create emphasis within an image. When executed well, it beautifully creates an added depth of field and richness to the photograph.

One way to create this effect quickly is to alter the image digitally using a blur. Here's a quick trick to create an optically "incorrect" image but a stunning example of selective emphasis:

1 Bring an image into your image editing program and create a copy of it onto a separate layer. Next, blur the entire image on the top layer.

2 Next, "erase" or remove a part of the blur, allowing the image (underneath) to show. By erasing the blur, you can carefully control what remains in focus and at greater detail. The red area (left) represents all of the top layer that remains blurred. The soft area around the face is the only part that remains in focus.

3 Your finished image has a subtle nuance between focus and blur.

I use this trick all the time.

WHY IT WORKS

The eye tends to look first at the sharpest part of the image. When you specifically create focus, you alter and direct how the image is read.

111

Effective Image Cropping

Narrative Choices

Cropping effectively can give you numerous choices within a single image. These choices will have significant impact on how the image is read and how it is ultimately perceived. These are conscious decisions that should be thought through. Here are a few things to consider when playing with the options:

> **Presentation and Format:** How will your image be presented? This will dictate your aspect ratio and ultimately your cropping decision.

> **Context:** Will this image be presented next to any other images? If so, you should consider the entire composition relative to the adjacent imagery (as in the sequence below).

> **The "Read":** Consider how your presentation will be viewed. Consider the entire composition. What you choose to eliminate is just as important as what you choose to keep.

If you learn nothing else, learn cropping well.

The original image, full frame.

The original image, presented in a sequence.

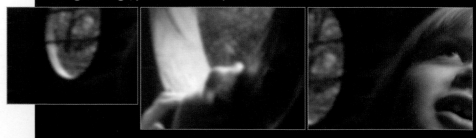

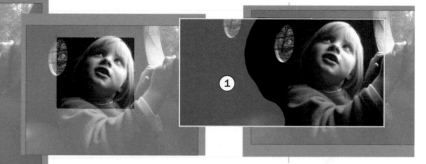

THE CINEMA ASPECT RATIO
This long horizontal aspect ratio invites all kinds of compositions. It's usually my first or second choice. I like to use it mostly for its read and its roots in film. There's a reason that all television is going into this wider format.

THE PORTRAIT
An intentional cropping over the face can draw a viewer into wanting more. These types of croppings usually imply that there is more to the image than is shown. Use this to your advantage to interest the viewer.

THE SQUARE
Symmetrical cropping has its roots in the old square-format cameras. I love it when a compositon works within a square. These images tend to feel a bit more formal due to their shape.

MAKING IT UP
Don't get frustrated if you're trying to crop into an image and run out of image. In some instances, you can paint or clone a background to complement your composition. The area in green ① was painted after the fact.

THE SEQUENTIAL STILL
This sequence uses only one source image, cropped using a variety of positions and sizes. The power of sequence puts each image next to the other, creating a filmstrip effect. This technique is great when you want to move the viewer through specific information in the image and when you want to create a longer composition.

Simple Image Processing

I've got about a dozen ways to resize images on my computer, but I often look for the quickest. Someone told me about Microsoft PowerToys on Microsoft.com. (Search for "PowerToys.") Look for the Image Resizer.

I've been seduced by the simplicity of "right-click."

The right-click menu is a very powerful way to process imagery in the context of selection. You might want to consider image size when you are going to e-mail someone or publish on the web. The software is getting smarter in re-sizing automatically, but you will want this type of control. Be sure to check which options are currently available in your right-click menu. Here are some quick and powerful tools found on right-click:

> **Send in E-Mail:** Available in different ways. From Microsoft Digital Image Library. Allows you to set the dimension and format of the mail.

> **Batch Edit in MiniLab:** Gives you flexibility. From Microsoft Digital Image Library. It automatically opens your images in Picture It! Digital Image Pro, allowing you to perform a multitude of image-processing steps. The output creates new files.

> **Convert File Format:** Gives you contextual control over the compression and file format of the image, creating a duplicate file in the desired format.

> **Open With:** Gives you access to any and all programs on your computer to specifically edit your images. I use this all the time.

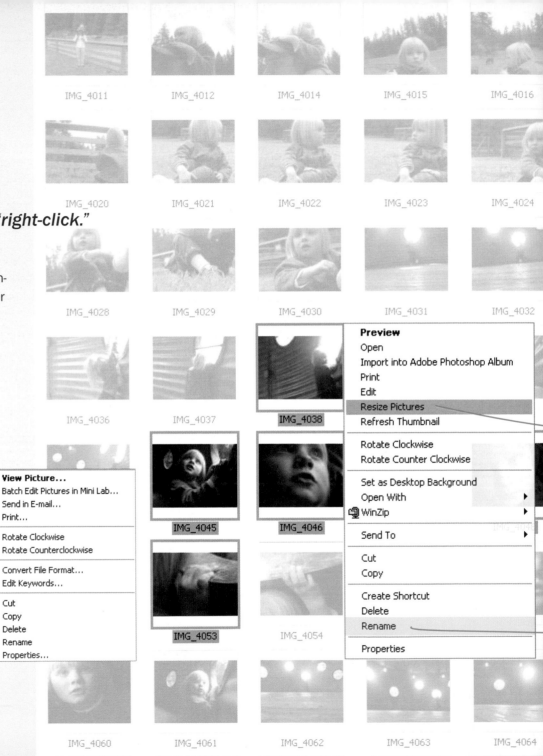

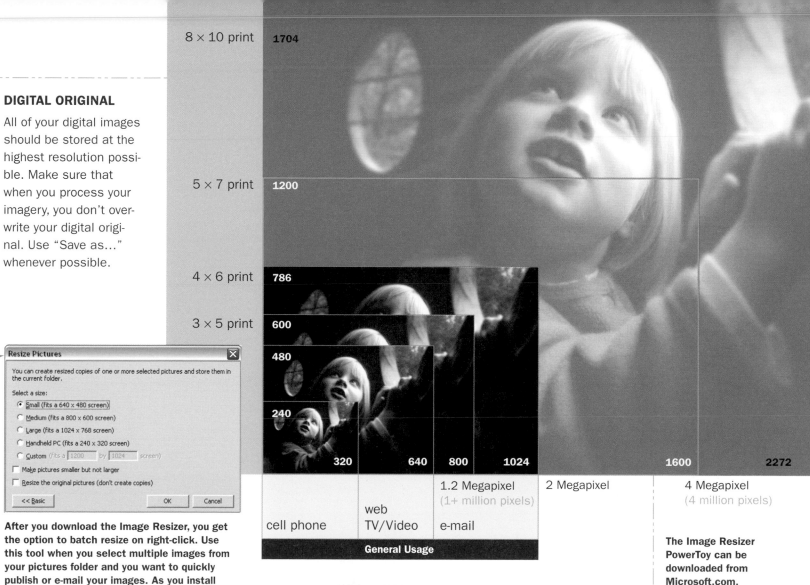

DIGITAL ORIGINAL

All of your digital images should be stored at the highest resolution possible. Make sure that when you process your imagery, you don't overwrite your digital original. Use "Save as…" whenever possible.

8 × 10 print — 1704

5 × 7 print — 1200

4 × 6 print — 786

3 × 5 print — 600

480

240

320   640   800   1024   1600   2272

1.2 Megapixel (1+ million pixels)   2 Megapixel   4 Megapixel (4 million pixels)

cell phone   web TV/Video   e-mail

General Usage

Resize Pictures

You can create resized copies of one or more selected pictures and store them in the current folder.

Select a size:
- ⊙ Small (fits a 640 x 480 screen)
- ○ Medium (fits a 800 x 600 screen)
- ○ Large (fits a 1024 x 768 screen)
- ○ Handheld PC (fits a 240 x 320 screen)
- ○ Custom (fits a 1200 by 1024 screen)

☐ Make pictures smaller but not larger
☐ Resize the original pictures (don't create copies)

<< Basic   OK   Cancel

After you download the Image Resizer, you get the option to batch resize on right-click. Use this tool when you select multiple images from your pictures folder and you want to quickly publish or e-mail your images. As you install other image editing software, monitor how they use this menu.

Many times you might want to batch rename your image files for searching or publishing purposes. Use "rename" when you need to rename multiple files at a time.

chloe (1).jpg   chloe (2).jpg   chloe (3).jpg   chloe (4).jpg

The Image Resizer PowerToy can be downloaded from Microsoft.com.

Image Resizer
 ImageResizer.exe
521 KB file
2 min @ 28.8 Kbps

115

Chapter Review

Effectively…

Human. You will always make decisions, regardless of automation, software, or annotation. You will make creative choices and build a body of work. Protect and preserve this work and enjoy its breadth and depth. You (and your audience) will enjoy the benefits of these decisions when looking back at the body of your work.

"We don't remember the days, we remember the moments."

Cesar Pavace

Effective Imagery Checklist

☐ Turn off that flash!

☐ Change your economics: Your cost per image should feel "free."

☐ Shoot more images: Edit them later.

☐ Think in sequential stills.

☐ Chase the light, not the location.

☐ Change your point of view.

☐ Crop for context.

section 3

Organizing Your Living Library

> **Life Building**

> **Organization**

> **Using Folders**

> **Easier Browsing and Retrieving**

> **Annotation and Keywording**

> **Location and Mapping**

> **Choosing What's Important**

> **Photo Editing**

"The two offices of memory are collection and distribution"

—Samuel Johnson

Life **Building**

Digital cameras will free you from the old economics of picture taking, but you can quickly inherit a new problem.

How do you organize the multitude of media on your computer?

To keep track of what you have and more effectively share memories, you need an approach to browse, organize, and distribute the images in your evergrowing digital library. You need a central place to store those images that currently feel "stuck" on your hard drive and to author those stories that are currently untold. I call this process "life building." It allows you to create a foundation and an approach defining how you think about organizing a living library of work that you will create, author, and share.

Let's begin your legacy…

Microsoft Digital Image Library gives you flexibility when organizing your media. You can view your images by folder, date, or keyword, producing results similar to those on the right. When you view by date, the images are organized automatically based on the date the image was taken. The other views are derived based on your own preferences.

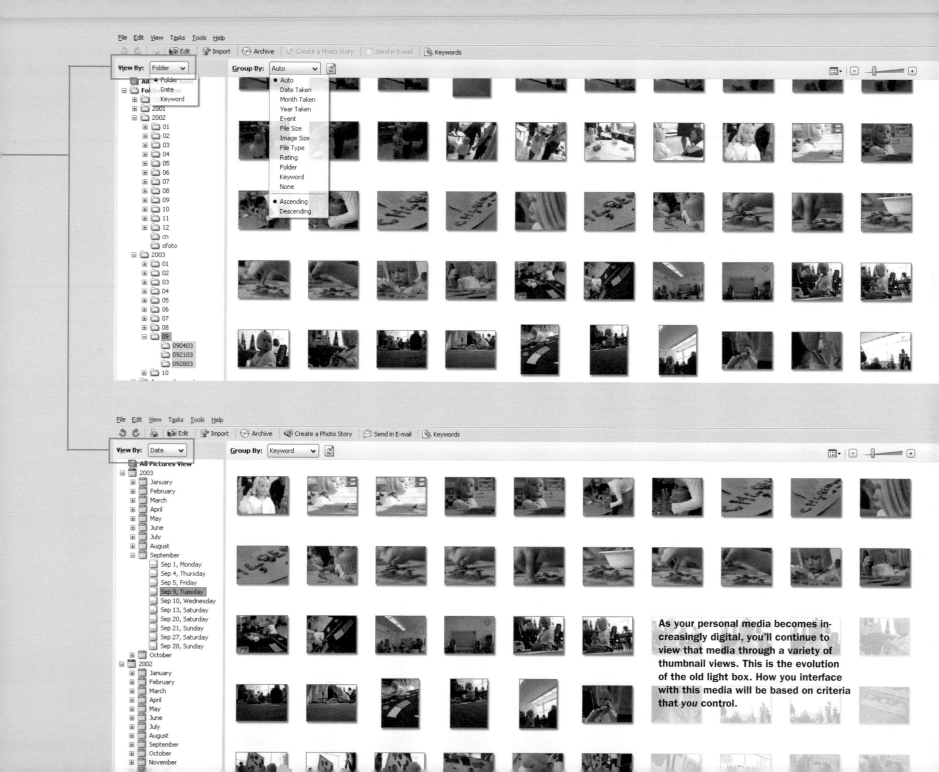

As your personal media becomes increasingly digital, you'll continue to view that media through a variety of thumbnail views. This is the evolution of the old light box. How you interface with this media will be based on criteria that *you* control.

In Microsoft Windows XP, the Folders button gives you immediate access to the folder heirarchy, making it easier to navigate the folder structure.

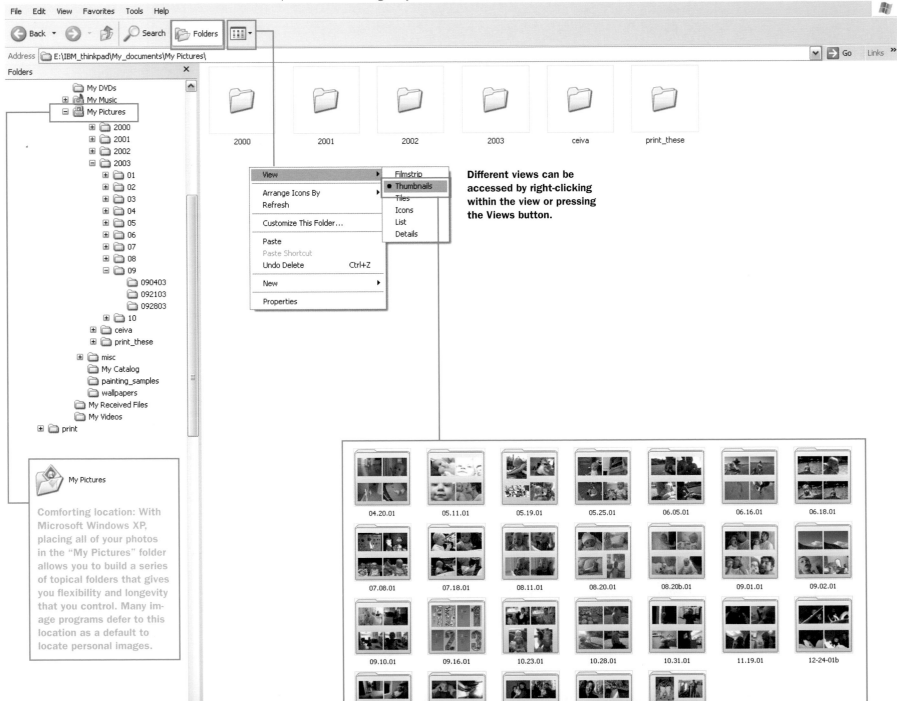

Different views can be accessed by right-clicking within the view or pressing the Views button.

Comforting location: With Microsoft Windows XP, placing all of your photos in the "My Pictures" folder allows you to build a series of topical folders that gives you flexibility and longevity that you control. Many image programs defer to this location as a default to locate personal images.

Creating a sustainable body of work should be fundamentally based on these key principles:

> **Organization**—You are the shopkeeper. You need the fastest and most efficient framework to access, browse, and author the inventory of media you will amass. The keywords you choose will define how your media will be organized and retrieved.

> **Selection**—You decide what is important. You need a criteria for making those keep/remove decisions when you craft your stories and build your memories both in-camera and on the computer.

Life building has a lot to do with editing and organization.

> **Automation**—You will develop swift, automatic tasks that will save you time. These tasks can help you automatically organize, prioritize, and author your memories, allowing you to integrate them into your daily schedule, so they become a more natural behavior.

The Thumbnail view in Windows XP gives you a hint of which images are inside that folder. If you hover your cursor over the thumbnail, it will display information about the contents.

> **Distribution**—You will author and share in multiple ways. Your living library will become a source from which you distribute a network of stories to multiple audiences. From traditional scrapbooks to DVDs, the approach you take to distribute and share your memories will become the foundation for your social network.

When browsing thumbnails, notice that you can preview both files and folders. Each will give a small representation of the image(s) contained within. The thumbnails are organized by alphanumeric order, so keep this in mind when naming your files and folders.

> **Preservation**—You are the protector of your media. The legacy of this work will rely on your ability to protect and preserve it. You should create a method to store, secure, and safeguard one of the most valuable assets you will ever create.

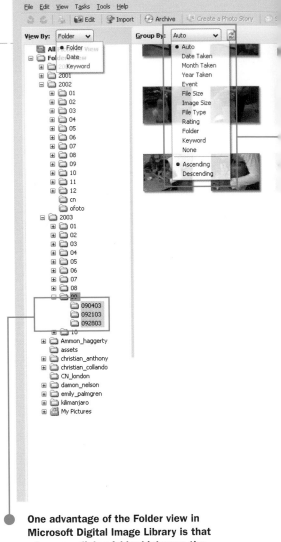

Organization: **The Shopkeeper in You...**

Good photo organization is like good shopkeeping because it requires the same skills as a good shopkeeper. If your store was meticulously clean, structured, and balanced and you had a fantastic photographic memory—would that be enough? Probably not.

In the past, the computer hasn't been that forgiving in organizing large amounts of personal media. It is very exacting in how it names, locates, and retrieves media. The way a computer organizes information relies heavily on your ability to remember how you are going to locate and retrieve it. In the past, if you happened to copy your images into a different location or folder than normal, your computer wouldn't have any idea that you were behaving differently. Your images would essentially be "lost," and you would have a frustrating experience retrieving them.

Image organization is improving...

I took 6000 images last year alone. Organizing them is a challenge.

One advantage of the Folder view in Microsoft Digital Image Library is that when you click a folder higher up the heirarchy, it displays every photo contained underneath it! This gives you the advantage of folders without diminishing the browsing experience.

Filter/view images by...

Interface

Digital image libraries now include a database model in addition to the folder model. What does that mean? Basically, the folders that you currently navigate are hierarchical, meaning that you reap most of the benefits of organization (logically named folders) when you browse their hierarchy (nested folders with lots of windows open at a time). Although the folders are sometimes cumbersome to navigate and view, there is a benefit to knowing that all of your images can be viewed in one location. Browsing photos, however, is cumbersome. For example, If you wanted to show someone the pictures of your son's first baseball game, you would have to remember the **date** it happened or the **topic** of folder you happened to put it in. You would have to do a lot of the work to locate, browse, and select. You would be the human catalog (sound familiar?).

In a database model, your search would extend to the entire group of media and images on your hard drive. It would look for keywords relating to either "baseball" or search by the dates on which you vaguely remember the event occurring. The interfaces that currently do this allow you to quickly scan and narrow the view to get your results. A folder model just can't do that. If your memory is bad, so will be your results.

The file and folder system (as you know it) won't go away entirely any time soon. Better file folder management will still be a very important topic personal media organization for a long time. The first to take advantage of the database structures will be applications, such as Adobe Photoshop Album and Microsoft Digital Image Library 9. Libraries of images created in those applications will ultimately be managed by the operating system itself.

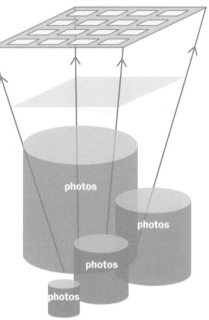

This rough diagram shows the fundamental difference in a database model of organization. The interface (in blue) is the display layer for the "buckets" of photos, (in green). When you change the view or filter, a different set of images are displayed. The size of the buckets can grow independently of the interface.

Once you've set your view, you can group the selection a number of ways. This gives you added flexibility when searching and browsing.

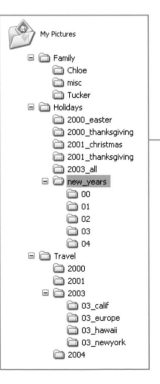

Using Folders: **Organization by Date vs. Topic**

When I ask most people how they organize their folders, they say, "I just throw them into the 'My Pictures' folder." There's a better way that isn't too complicated and doesn't take up too much time.

If you rely on file folders to both organize and retrieve your images, one way to do it is to create a simple hierarchy of folders, organized by date or by topic. I've seen variations done either way, but most of the people I've interviewed find that if they shoot a lot of images, the following organizations seem to be the most efficient.

In both of these examples, there is a lot of flexibility in how you create and name your folders. Notice how "New_Years" is treated differently. You might have certain topics that require more granularity than others. The primary rule I've learned is that once you start with one organization system, stick with it! Don't change midway through.

Example1: Organize Broadly by **Date**, Specific by Topic

The date file structure is the one I use the most. It works for me, simply because I like a stronger emphasis on date than on topic when using folders. This is also a very flexible structure. In this model, there is a folder that represents year, month, and (sometimes) day. Each is a folder within the hierarchy. Depending on the amount of media I produce, the granularity can change. For example, sometimes I only copy two large photo sessions in a single month. Instead of choosing to add another layer of hierarchy, I'll just create a folder that relates the topic of the photos contained within it.

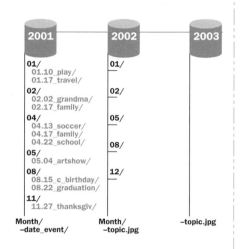

Example of three different ways to group media by date>topic

Example2: Organize Broadly by **Topic**, Specific by Date

In the topic file structure, a series of broad topics organized by folder are created at the top level. These topics are chosen specifically as recurring themes. They might be locations, places, or people, for example. They are organized specifically to aid in retrieval. Media organized this way is easier to retrieve *if* you've named your folders correctly and placed the media correctly. I have some friends that use this model and love it. As the folders get deeper, so do the topics. The topics are then dated to distinguish between topics.

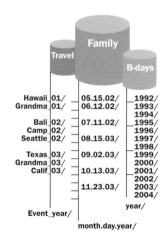

Example of three different ways to group media by topic>date

My Pictures | **Click + Hold (Shift) + Double-Click**

Easier **Browsing and Retrieving**

Despite how you organize your folders, there has long been a need to quickly and easily browse many files and folders at once. I have found that the Folders view in Microsoft Windows XP is the easiest. I mention it only because it was a revelation when someone told me how to do this a couple of years ago. It's easy to do. As an example, navigate to the "My Pictures" folder on your machine. When you double-click the folder, also hold down the Shift key; this will open a new two-pane window that will allow you to quickly navigate the hierarchy on the left pane and view the files in the right pane. In Windows XP, you can also press the Folders button at the top of the window. With the Explorer Bar set to Folders, I quickly make this window full screen when I need to do heavy browsing and retrieving between multiple folders. This view is also the best way to test your organizational folder structure.

When I browse and retrieve images in Windows XP, I use different views for different tasks. By right-clicking within the window, it is really quick to change the view. The Thumbnail view (this page) is great for looking at images in sequence and previewing detail within images. The Folder view (facing page) is used to navigate across multiple folders.

The Folders button also gives you immediate access to the folder heirarchy, making it easier to navigate the folder structure.

eric_cheng
- kilimanjaro
  - Equipment
  - Gallery
  - Itinerary
    - Day1
    - Day2
    - Day3
    - Day4
    - Day5
    - Day6
    - Day7
    - Day8
    - Day9
  - Participants
  - Preparation
- pics

This example illustrates that file hierarchy can also contribute to the organization of how that content is experienced. The folder structure here mimicks the organization of a site, which was later published. Use this technique when planning specific media for publishing or sharing together.

echeng.com presents

KILIMANJARO

A MT. KILIMANJARO RESOURCE PAGE - MACHAME ROUTE

introduction   preparation   participants   itinerary   thoughts   medication   tips   equipment   gallery   resources & link

INTRODUCTION

On January 5th, 2001, two friends and I departed the San Francisco Bay Area for Tanzania to climb Mt. Kilimanjaro. When asked why I climbed the mountain, my usual answer is, "Uh... I don't know...", because my discovery Kilimanjaro was pure serendipity (my friend Munira had made the initial suggestion, but was later unable to go). I roped Wally into the trip by buying him an airplane ticket, and Margo became interested after the trip came up randomly at work one day.

I've heard Mt. Kilimanjaro called the "most underestimated mountain in the world." It's nicknamed "the mountain that glitters" and "the place where God lives". Most people think it's easy because it's not a technical climb; after all, it's simply a hike straight up and down (more or less) the mountain. However, as we discovered, the effects of fatigue and altitude were very real. Luckily, my friends were very supportive prior to my trip: "You're insane," "You're going to die," "Can I have your car"... ah, I love having supportive friends. Here a good page detailing high altitude sickness...

SECTION VISUALS

mt. kilimanjaro, from springland b&b hotel

VISUALS PAGE 1 OF 5

Location and Travels: Kilimanjaro

by Eric Cheng
Software Engineer, Musician, & Underwater Photographer

In January of 2001, I climbed Mt. Kilimanjaro. Not being a regular mountain climber, I felt lost in dealing with the preparation necessary for a successful climb to the summit, and I really had no idea what to expect before arriving at the base of the mountain. I did a bit of web research and read a book about the climb, but I always felt like the accounts weren't personal or exhaustive enough to satisfy my curiosity. And so, in the back of my mind, I set out to document my climb in a way that would be rewarding for both me and others who might be interested in the experience.

During the trip, I kept a handwritten journal and took digital pictures of just about everything I saw. I knew that I would eventually be assembling the information in a more organized fashion, but I really didn't bother to organize it explicitly for two reasons: 1) There was no outlet electricity, and 2) I wanted to have an "immersive" experience without the confines of obligatory documentation. I think of what I did as collecting "raw material," without sacrificing the opportunity to experience the majesty around me. But that doesn't mean I wasn't thorough. I always took the time to pull out my camera when I thought something was beautiful, and I took the time to photograph and write about almost everything that caught my eye. I enjoyed keeping a journal in the field because memories were still vivid in my mind as I committed them to paper.

When I returned home, I started to organize my images. I divided up what I had captured—both images and words—into areas that documented the chronology of the climb (day 1, day 2, and so on) and into areas that documented more abstract ideas (such as preparation, equipment, and concluding thoughts). The resulting organization was simple and included photographs, entries copied verbatim from my field journal, and reflective comments interspersed throughout. Taking the time to add thoughts to my field journal allowed me to fill in the holes I had left and to comment more objectively about the frame of mind I was in while on the mountain. Writing more about the trip was also great because it gave me a chance to reflect on the experience I had just been through.

Eric's Kilimanjaro journal can be found at:
www.echeng.com/travel/kilimanjaro

...I started to organize my images into areas that documented chronology and more abstract ideas...

I set out to document my climb in a way that would be rewarding for both me and others who might be interested in the experience.

Group By: | Auto ▾ | ⟳

- ● Auto
- Date Taken
- Month Taken
- Year Taken
- Event
- File Size
- Image Size
- File Type
- Rating
- Folder
- **Keyword**
- None

- ● Ascending
- Descending

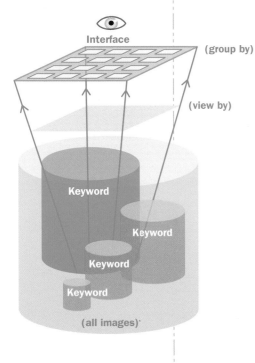

👁
Interface

(group by)

(view by)

Keyword

Keyword

Keyword

Keyword

(all images)·

Annotation and Keywording

Imagine, for example, what it would be like to put all of your images into one big bucket. Imagine there is a tiny little Post-It Note attached to the back of each picture. On each Post-It is written different attributes or characteristics of that image. The rules of the bucket require that each time you reach into it you need to say what you are looking for. Every picture with a Post-It on the back that had a match would immediately be put into your hand.

When images are captured with a digital camera, a series of information tags are also captured—like the Post-It notes attached to the pictures in your bucket. This "tagged" information, called "metadata," is inserted into the file that your camera outputs as a digital photo and follows the file around. It starts with an accurate time stamp, noting when the media was captured. From there, it may include any number of other characteristics about how the image and what kind of settings on the camera were part of capturing the image, such as the camera make and model, the time when the photo was shot, and the aperture settings.

Keywording (also called "annotation") creates virtual buckets of associated images. The blue bucket in the diagram represents a view that has been assigned only to one keyword. Viewing can include one or multiple keywords.

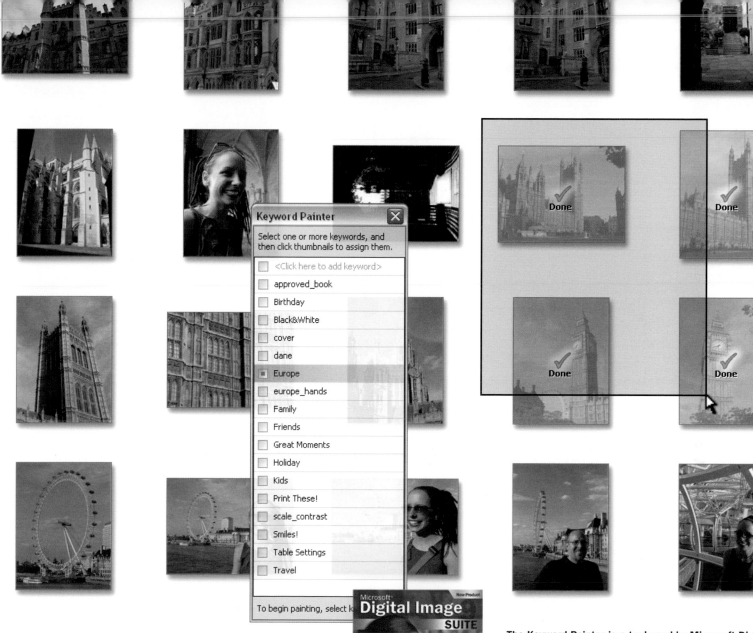

The Keyword Painter is a tool used by Microsoft Digital Image Library. This makes browsing and keywording a seamless process. By using keywords and metadata with the photos, you can begin to create your own categories and groupings of photos. This allows you to automatically search for specific types of images.

Keywording Using Adobe Photoshop Album

Importing images from a digital camera into a digital image library should automatically log When (time and date) when those images were authored. This is called the "time stamp." Time stamping is helpful because you can automatically sort all of the files based on date right away. Once you are able to view by date, you can begin to use keywords to bring additional context and focus to your ever-increasng library.

Each program may have a different way of applying the keywords, but most allow you to apply a single keyword to multiple selections at a time. Adobe Photoshop Album uses a tagging interface.

Here are a few things to keep in mind when keywording:

> **Add the "Where":** A time stamp combined with a location is a fundamental orientation for a narrative. Establish your keywords in a way that allow you to create cross-groupings by the locations of the images.

> **Add the "Who":** Adding keywords to a large number of photos can be done quickly to reflect social interactions between the people you know. Use this with time or location. You can also add keyword tags to identify multiple people in a single photograph.

> **Add the "Why":** This is harder to do, but when you can create a causal relationship between your media and its meaning, the keyword can be very significant, especially when combined with other keyword categories. An example of this type of information could be "Firsts"—for example, if your son or daughter begins to crawl for the first time, you might want to categorize that with a common word along with time or location.

TRY AN EMOTION

Take a pass at adding an emotional tag to those images that strike you as significant. You might benefit from looking up images later that speak to a word or phrase that represents a particular type of emotion. This is a different kind of approach than just adding the facts. It allows you to isolate those images that are distinctly unique from the rest based on an emotional context.

Adobe Photoshop Album has a distinct Timeline view that allows you to view your media by volume and time.

Adding keywords in Adobe Photoshop Album is a great exercise that helps you think about how to describe images and group them.

For my library, I have created a couple of unique tags. I have a keyword I use called "Wonder." It represents all of those images of my son or daughter that represent growth and marvel as they grow.

Group by: Auto ⌄

● Auto
Date Taken
Month Taken
Year Taken
Event
File Size
Image Size
File Type
Rating
Folder
Keyword
None

● Ascending
Descending

< Laughter >

Microsoft Digital Image Library allows me to group my images by keyword. One of my favorite keyword tags is "Laughter." This is a remarkable way to conjure great memories when browsing and authoring. It always seems to make me smile.

The Big Bucket

Instead of creating a series of folders for organizing pictures, more and more image library programs (such as Microsoft Digital Image Library and Adobe Photoshop Album) are using a database approach to handle the management and organization for you. These programs treat your media like a big database (bucket) that can be infinitely sorted based on attached metadata. The software automatically performs certain tasks, but it gives you the flexibility to add new groupings of photos based on time, place, location, subject, or any additional topic you create. Some of this information is already available on the images you take, and some programs allow you to add this metadata onto your media. The richer the information is, the more you can leverage your library.

Imagine that you've selected a close-up image of your subject that you like, and you want to find others that are similar (by selecting Find Similar). By using the keywords you specify, the computer can quickly identify other photographs and display very intuitively accurate representations of images that you ask for. You can also choose a photograph by a particular date and ask your software to display all of the photographs taken within a certain number of days of when that image was taken. The use of metatags with imagery is still in its infancy, but the practice is growing quickly as digital cameras and software learn to take advantage of this rich information that includes time, location, and any additional contextual information relevant to the image.

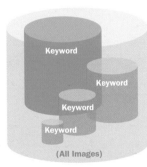

Keyword
Keyword
Keyword
Keyword
(All Images)

Adding keywords is a great exercise that helps you think about how to describe your images and group them.

The Facets of Your Media

One of the key advantages of a digital image catalog is the ability to view the same material in multiple ways. It's like looking at a polished gem with many facets. Each surface becomes a view into the heart of the stone. There has been an explosion of image organization software. Your media is the prize that these software programs fight for. New innovative views take advantage a multitude of keyword attributes that you can filter and control. Here are just a few of the existing views that programs provide:

> **View by Date (year, month, day):** This view is tremendously helpful. You can quickly view images by year, month, or day by quickly selecting the appropriate view.

> **View Enlarge/Reduce Thumbnails (on the fly):** This view might seem like a small detail, but I've found that the ability to change the size of the thumbnail quickly is enormously helpful.

> **View by Keyword:** This view is an enormously helpful way for me to query my image library and look for specific types of photos.

> **View by Folder:** Many times the mental model of images by folder is exactly what I need. Having access to the folder structure within my library is fantastic.

> **View by Location:** New views offered by your digital image library show your personal media based on location information. You will find location information increasingly available to you when authoring media.

The Calendar view in Adobe Photoshop Album is a great way to zoom in and out of time. The interface allows you to view by year, month, or day. This is an example of views that are generated automatically for you.

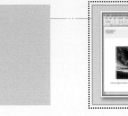

View Picture...
Edit Picture...
Send in E-mail...
Print...

Rotate Clockwise
Rotate Counterclockwise

Find Similar Picture
Go to Picture Location

Convert File Format...
Edit Keywords...

Cut
Copy
Delete
Rename
Properties...

Annotation is Context

by Ammon Haggerty
Designer/Engineer, Photographer, Taxonomist, & Disc Jockey

A common practice when people share images is to include with the image some sort of description, which helps define meaning. This description, or "subject metadata," is the most common form of story telling and contextualizing. Although describing the meaning of the photo can be the most useful way to connect meaning to an image, it can also be labor intensive and is often the barrier which prevents sharing in the first place.

Sharing images without context breaks one of the primary rules of storytelling. To tell a story, you need to have meaning, and to have meaning, you need context. Context is the thread connecting one photo to another. So the question is: How do you create context without the laborious process of describing each image in detail?

Creating a context doesn't have to be personal or even literal. The goal is to create enough meaning so that the viewer can understand why an image exists and what it has to do with the story being told. If the story is about an adventure to the beach, much of the story could be about the journey. Journeys often involve movement, which is a product of change in space and time. Space and time are terrific tools in telling an interesting story—who went where, for how long, and how far.

Space and time information happens to be an easy commodity to share. Time is often captured by the camera device, and location is information one can usually remember when reviewing the images. So now, with time and location information, you are able to tell part of the story without any personal description.

In this example, viewing the image properties in Microsoft Digital Image Library can reveal some valuable context about the image. These properties can be included when the image is published to provide a richer context and narrative to the image.

The big unknowns are usually "why" and "where." These usually need to be added manually. The caption under Robert's photo provides the user with a better understanding of why the car is parked, where the event has taken place, and the events which will follow.

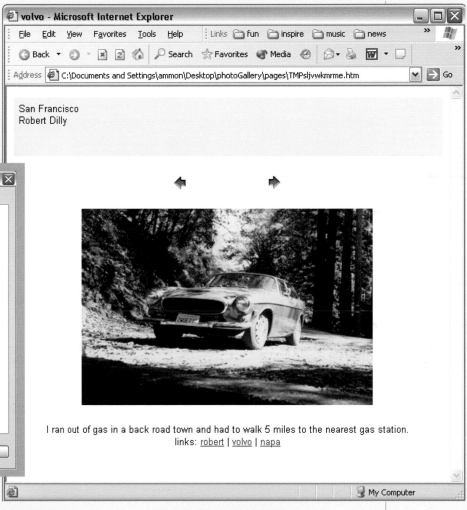

volvo.jpg Properties

General | Camera settings

File Name: volvo

Location: E:\IBM_thinkpad\My_documents\book\PR...\mapping
Type of File: JPEG Image
Size: 165 KB (169,852 bytes)
Width: 640 pixels DPI: 72
Height: 686 pixels Bit Depth: 24

Date Taken: Tuesday , October 21, 2003
Time Taken: 11:10:21 AM
Modified: Tuesday, October 21 2003 11:10 PM
Last Archived:
Caption: volvo
Description: I ran out of gas in the back road town and had to walk 5 miles to the nearest gas station
Author: Robert Dilly
Keywords: <Click here to assign keywords to this picture>
Rating: ★ ★ ★ ☆ ☆

OK | Cancel

San Francisco
Robert Dilly

I ran out of gas in a back road town and had to walk 5 miles to the nearest gas station.
links: <u>robert</u> | <u>volvo</u> | <u>napa</u>

This HTML template exposes the keywords as hyperlinks. This creates a network of connected stories and additional information automatically. Using annotations provides you with rich opportunities for authoring throughout the life of your media.

1 item selected

File Name: volvo.jpg
Caption: volvo
Date Taken: Tuesday, October 21, 2003   11:10 AM
Keywords: volvo, robert, napa
Rating: ★ ★ ★ ☆ ☆
File Size: 165 KB
Image Size: 640 x 686 (Smaller)

Location and Mapping: Orientation by Location

Strong memories can be triggered by a location or a map. If we don't remember the date, we'll most certainly remember the place. Therefore, two pieces of metadata provide the context of a photo: the time stamp (the date and time), plus the geographic location. Knowing that a photo was taken on your birthday last year, for example, or that a photo was taken at Disneyland, says a lot about the photo even before you see a single pixel. If you think a bit about your favorite photographs, there's a good chance that time, place, or both immediately come to mind. In many cases, you'll associate photos with an event, such as "John and Mary's wedding," but events themselves are defined by where and when they happened.

So, how do we go about acquiring location information?

What do we do with it once we have it?

In the physical world, a common cure for disorientation is the use of a map. Maps are a universal tool for understanding spatial orientation and transcending language and culture.

golden gate park

SAN FRANCISCO

legend

✛ map link　　◻ photo　　⊟ video　　◁ audio　　◪ text　　◯ web link　　△ info

Courtesy of The General Libraries, The University of Texas at Austin. Mapping and location interface by Ammon Haggerty.

Mapping: The Universal Language

by Ammon Haggerty
Designer/Engineer, Photographer, Taxonomist, & Disc Jockey

Orientation is a common oversight in the digital realm. A viewing experience without orientation can have negative consequences, such as a lack of understanding. In the physical world, a common cure for disorientation is the use of a map. Maps are a universal tool for understanding spatial orientation and transcending language and culture.

The word "map" generally conjures an image of geographic cities and countries, but the world of "mapping" extends far beyond the bounds of physical space. Maps are used in all aspects of life to orient and organize our lives—some examples include: flow charts, housing plans, and family trees.

So, you might be wondering how maps can used in sharing your personal experiences. Maps represent location, which is a powerful tool for storytelling. When the user knows where an event took place, they become better oriented to the experience and have a better understanding of the context and how it relates to you. Maps also encourage exploration by their very nature—people can't help but orient themselves with the map.

A simple mapping example might consist of a geographic map combined with photos you have recently taken. To make them cohesive, add links from the map to the photos. The end result allows the user to understand how one photo relates to another and gives a better understanding of the physical space where the photos reside.

Here are three examples of how mapping could be used.

In this example from Qaswa.com, the display of the photographs is adjacent to the maps. The maps that are used range from hand-drawn maps to those acquired on the trip.

Example 1: The Family Tree

Jeff wanted to assemble a photo collection of all his immediate relatives, and then post it on his website for all his relatives. Once Jeff collected and scanned all the photos, he was left with the task of identifying and labeling all the members of the family.

The approach often taken is to describe each person's relationship with the rest of the family. The photo then has a description like "Great-Great-Grandpa Joe Smith, father of Jeff's mothers' fathers' father." While the description works, the overall orientation to relationships begins to fall apart.

Here's a situation in which a map can provide orientation. Let's take the same scenario, this time creating a simple family tree map—like the one everyone has in their baby book.

Now, mapping links to the tree elements provides a way to show the photos or images of each family member, while providing the hierarchy needed to understand the members' overall relationships.

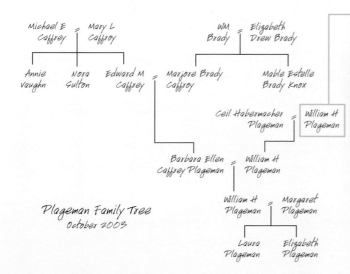

This simple example creates both a spatial relationship with the photos as well as a context. As the author, you can quickly fill out the map in a way that shows how "complete" your project has become, filling in the photos as you find them.

Example 2: Vacation in San Francisco

Michael and Lisa went to San Francisco during their summer vacation. They shared the duty of documenting the trip with their digital camera. When they were in San Francisco, they bought a Bay Area map to help them get around and then kept the map as memorabilia when they returned.

Michael and Lisa noticed the unique orientation of the San Francisco and the surrounding towns and wanted to capture the feeling of seeing the city from the many views and perspectives in their presentation.

They scanned the Bay Area map to use as a base image for the photo gallery. Then they added reference links to the map showing the location and direction of where they were standing when they took the photos. They also colored the links according to who took the photo so that one could, at a glance, know if the photo was taken by Michael or Lisa. Because they used a digital camera which captures a time stamp, they added time and date references to each link.

Now, the user can look at the map and follow the couple on their journey around the San Francisco Bay area. Each photo better orients the viewer to the space while allowing the viewer the freedom to explore the journey in a nonlinear manner.

GPS devices can also be used to accurately derive location information.

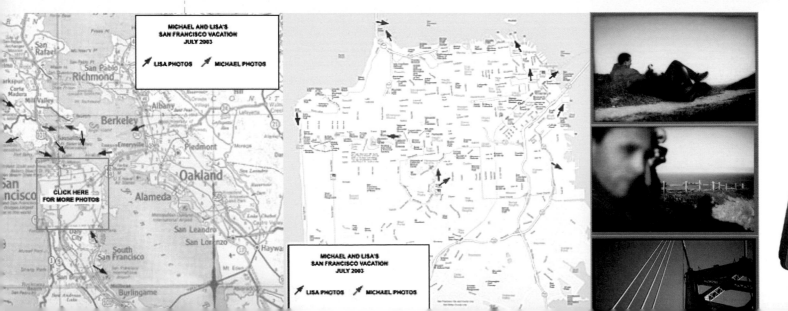

Example 3: Laura's House

Laura just bought a new house in Portland. She was excited to show her family back in New York her new property and wanted them to get a feel for the neighborhood as well. With her digital camera, she took dozens of photos from all angles both inside and out.

Laura received the blueprints of the house with the purchase, so she decided to use the layout to help describe the space. She then mapped each photo to the blueprints, which saved her a great deal of time writing descriptions of the rooms and their orientations.

Laura liked the results, but she wanted an even more realistic experience for her family. She used the photo of the front of the house and mapped photo links to all the areas she could see in the photo. She turned some of the linked photos into additional maps. The end result is a "virtual walk-through" of her new house.

In this example, the floor plan of the house is used to create an index for specific photos that were taken when walking throughout the house.

143

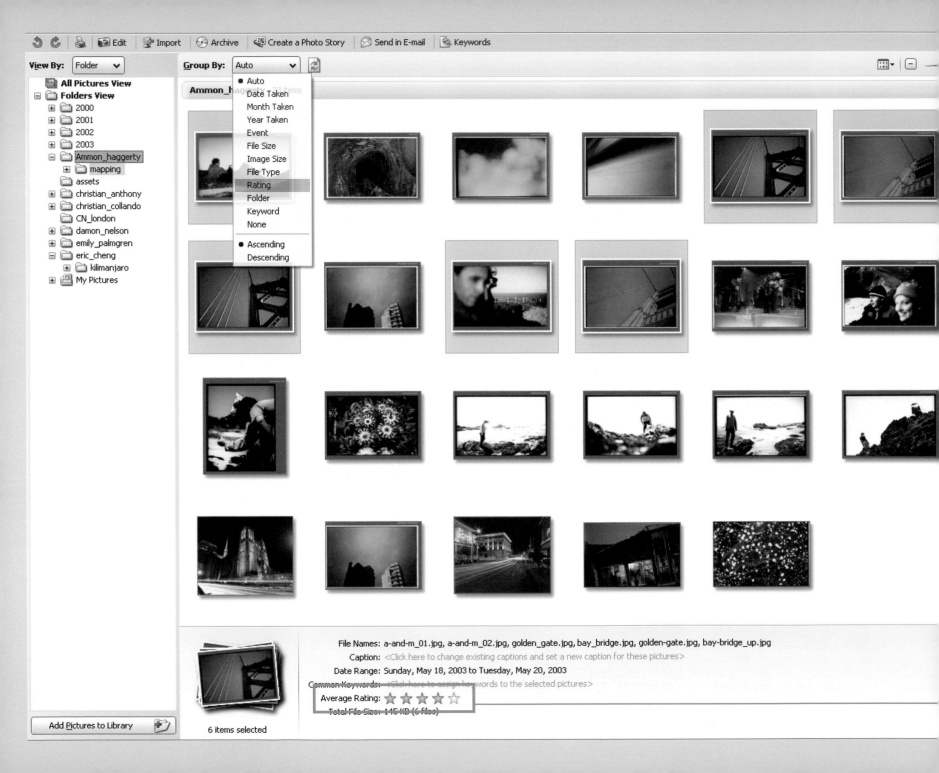

Choosing What's Important

There's an exercise called "Lifeboating" that forces you to edit down to the bare essence of what you find the most valuable.

If you had to keep just a fraction of your memories, what would you keep? This is a tough question.

What would you keep in your lifeboat?

No matter how well organized your images are, you must edit constantly. This requires making choices. You ultimately choose what to keep and delete, but I like to think of it rather as a matter of focus. **When you explicitly delete an image, it is gone forever. When you de-emphasize it, the image is removed from view.** Whether you choose to make these choices on your camera or in your computer, I suggest that you preserve the integrity of what will ultimately be your digital original. Try not to delete an image unless you are absolutely sure that you will never need to use it again.

Digital storage is an increasingly cheaper resource. When making decisions in your image library, I suggest selecting "favorites" based on a ranking system rather than deleting the media altogether. You never know how I might want to use those images later.

> **One way to photo-edit is to explicitly label your "favorite" images using the Rating stars in Microsoft Digital Image Library. This allows you to create editorial focus without deleting. You can then group your photos using the rating system.**

Photo Editing: Making Those Personal Choices

Once you've captured a lot of material, you need to select and edit it effectively. Let's face it; you don't have a lot of time to do this, so knowing how to edit quickly and effectively is very important. If you look at how choosing and regrouping images is done in other publishing mediums, they usually separate the photographer from the final editing process. This makes sense because a photographer tends to believe that most or all of the images are keepers. Don't make this mistake. Chances are that your audience won't have the time to view all of the images either. It makes more work for you and for them.

Good photo editing is a combination of skill and having the right tools. Professional editors have a keen eye for choosing and grouping images that can either sell products or tell stories. They usually operate within defined parameters to answer a specific question or illustrate a design problem. It is both a skill and a developed personal style.

Photographs are usually selected with a story in mind. That story might not yet be complete, but the process of selection will help shape the story that it becomes.

In the example below, a story started with four images, but was reduced to two. Creative cropping, ordering, and image flipping depicts a simple day at the beach. The bridge helps orient the location of the trip. The focus on the bridge suggests that the journey was just as significant as the destination.

10.23.02

On Saturday we went across the bridge...   spent the day at the beach...   and then came home. Wish U were there.

When selecting images for a story or sequence, look for color consistency, similar shapes, and a distinct sense of direction. Every image you choose should have a place in the sequence and an order that contributes to the story.

Selection. **Naturally...**

To edit your own photographs, try working with a context. This will help guide the process, and it will also expose your process.

Ask yourself:

> Do the photographs look good together?

> Do they communicate what I'm trying to say?

> Is the image quality effective in this context?

Try to view many images grouped together, and, if you can, move them around and group them in different ways. With traditional prints, this would be done by laying them out on a large flat table. With color slides or transparencies, you would lay them out over a light table. There are many tricks that allow you to quickly and efficiently browse and select your images when photo editing on a computer.

When searching for images, the Microsoft Digital Image Library allows you to right-click an image to "find similar"—this will automatically search and display similar images.

Here are a few helpful techniques for browsing and selecting photographs for your stories:

> **Look for Patterns:** Images in a sequence reveal interesting patterns of both color and shape. You can position a close-up against a long shot. You can alternate "people" images with "place" images. You can also unify a series of images by color or shape alone. An easy way to do this is to choose all the close-up images of your subject with good expressions. Another way to look for patterns is to "crop into" a single image, essentially creating "new" images in the process. You'll find that when you focus on specific areas of a shot by cropping them and reframing them, you'll discover a wealth of new images. Grab 20 of them from the same shot, and see what happens!

> **Use odd numbers:** I can't explain why this works, but using groups of three or five images produces more interesting sequences than groups of two or four.

> **Force limitations:** I do this all the time. "Less is more" here. Ask yourself if you can tell the entire story in one to three images. This will really force you to get to the essence of the story. Another

great way to force limitation is to select images only within a particular time frame, color range, or location. This can focus your attention on specific aspects of images with similar characteristics. I find myself often deciding which images I will choose based on strict limitations. This makes photo-editing easier and allows me to author more quickly.

> **Choose something at random:** Close your eyes and grab an image. It's an exercise in fate. Much like a grab bag, it forces you to pretend that this is the only image of the bunch. This forced choice makes you put more emphasis on describing the image than on trying to show it. Many times this is a good thing.

> **Take a screenshot:** I do this all the time. When browsing, if you like what you see, take a screenshot. On a PC, pressing (Alt + Prt Scrn) will take a copy of whatever is your current window at that moment. Paste it into your image program, crop it, and save it as an image. I use this to create new images all the time.

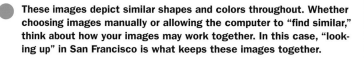

These images depict similar shapes and colors throughout. Whether choosing images manually or allowing the computer to "find similar," think about how your images may work together. In this case, "looking up" in San Francisco is what keeps these images together.

Chapter Review

Effectively…

Structured. Life building refers to both the process and the library used for storing images. It can become the source of some of your most treasured memories and the foundation for the legacy that you share with others. Structure your library enough to remind you of the context of your events, but don't let your library structure you out of the joy of keeping it around.

> *"The great use of life is to spend it for something that will outlast it."*
>
> *William James*

Living Library: Checklist

☐ Organize and centralize your media.

☐ Choose a folder structure that works for you.

☐ *Stick with that structure!*

☐ Identify your keywords and topics.

☐ Use location and map whenever possible.

☐ Photo-edit with your "life boat" in mind.

☐ Don't forget to archive!

section 4
Sharing Your Memories

> **The Share Map**

> **Hard Copies**

>> **Conventional Prints**

>> **Professional Prints**

>> **Custom Prints and Collage**

> **Soft Copies**

>> **Effective E-Mail**

>> **Slide Shows and Presentations**

>> **Movies and Media**

>> **Dynamic Media**

> **Increasingly Mobile Memories**

"Memories of our lives, of our works and our deeds will continue on in others."

—Rosa Parks

A single image can have multiple uses. From a 4 × 6 print to a website, your digital original may be shown across multiple media and audiences. My siblings often enjoy the website, but my grandparents get prints.

Sharing **Your Memories**

Distributing and sharing your memories is an exciting and prolific topic and is the basis for provoking all kinds of new experiences, products, and interactions.

Sharing your memories should be the most fun you have with your media.

"To share" also means to allocate, assign, allot, deliver, circulate, spread, disseminate, scatter, give out, and supply. These words can invoke ideas on how an image or a sequence of images is experienced and distributed. These experiences will always rely on a delivery method and format.

A printed book may have a very different use than an e-mail message or a dynamic slide show or movie. To optimize each experience to the most appropriate format, you have to understand the benefits and interrelationships between them.

"No memory is ever alone; it's at the end of memories, a dozen trails that each have their own associations."

Louis L'Amour

Find ways to showcase your images using slide shows and screensavers when your laptop or PC screen is not in use. In this example, a Tablet PC is set on a picture stand to become an instant digital picture frame.

The Share Map

It is no surprise that a significant addition to sharing photos is through the Internet. This is coupled with a prolific number of new and exciting electronic devices and color display screens. In the past five years, the cost of color displays has gone down, allowing for increasing opportunities to afford and distribute digital "soft copies" of our memories.

The format(s) you choose will dictate how the images are communicated. For the sake of simplicity, I'll suggest that these are grouped into two main categories: Hard Copy and Soft Copy.

Just a few years ago, it would have seemed impossible to speak with someone on your cell phone while you took a picture and sent it to the person via the same phone you were speaking on. Today the act of sharing is closely coupled with authoring. When you imagine the types of images that you will want to distribute and share, imagine a diversified body of work that you build and distribute for both hard *and* soft copy.

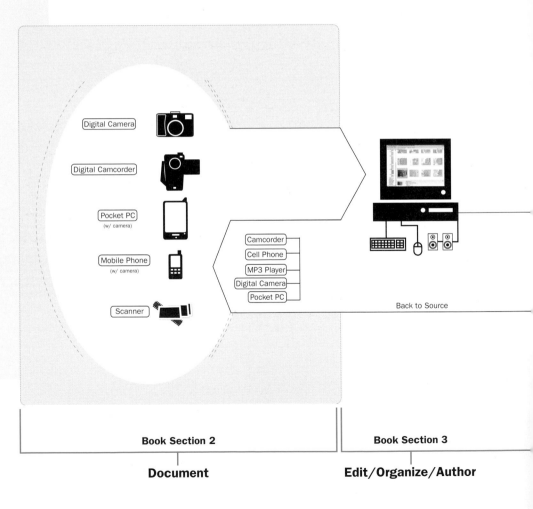

Digital Camera

Digital Camcorder

Pocket PC
(w/ camera)

Mobile Phone
(w/ camera)

Scanner

Camcorder
Cell Phone
MP3 Player
Digital Camera
Pocket PC

Back to Source

Book Section 2

Book Section 3

Document

Edit/Organize/Author

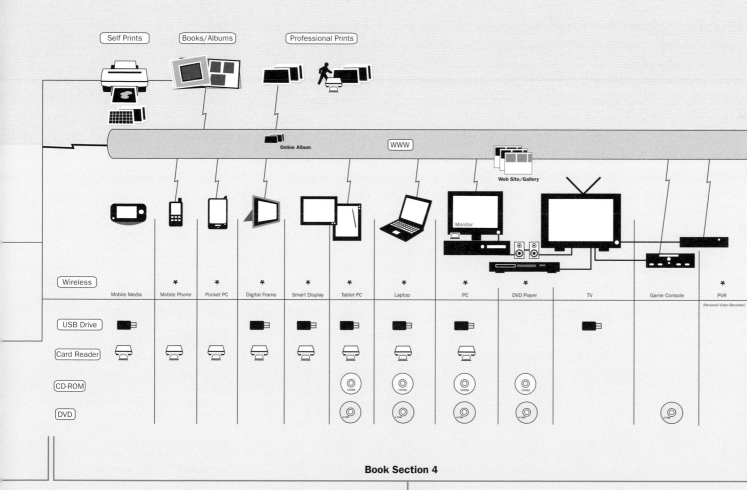

HARD COPY

These formats rely on a physical representation of the image or sequence. These range (greatly) in resolution, quality, and form. They can be traditional 4×6 glossy prints, a custom color print book, a scrapbook, or even a coffee mug. Hard copies are the most traditional and often the most widely known in memory making. Hard copies usually tend to memorialize the media.

SOFT COPY

These presentations allow an image or a sequence to be shared digitally (through e-mail, instant message, DVD, mobile phones, or the web). Many of these formats allow for a richer multimedia experience using motion and/or sound. They can be copied and shared in greater numbers. At the heart of any soft copy is the flexibility for multiple uses and impressions. Soft copies usually capture the immediacy, or the temporal qualities, of the media.

Book Section 4

Share

Hard **Copies**

"I'd buy your book if you would only show me how I could get 4 × 6 prints made easily and cost effectively."

Every mother I spoke to

A big misconception about digital photography is that you have to give up your hard-copy prints. A common problem is that too many photos get on the computer, and not enough of the "keepers" are printed. There are a lot of areas for possible confusion and concern about printing, but the most significant problems arise around quality and price. To help you, I've put anything that is related to printing into two basic categories:

> **Conventional Prints.** These are prints that you can make at home. You can quickly and easily output a number of images on a standard-sized piece of paper using a common template. For many popular home printers, making great photos is a simple process of optimizing some settings and taking some fairly easy trial and error steps. For every conventional print you make, an important evaluation is made about the proposed use and longevity of the image versus its cost and convenience.

> **Professional Prints.** These images are printed by a photo lab (like you used to do with your film cameras). More and more photo labs are becoming proficient at printing from a digital image. The quality is usually higher than prints made at home, and so is the cost per print. The cost can range greatly depending on whom you use, but the professional prints can reflect the same quality you get from traditional film cameras.

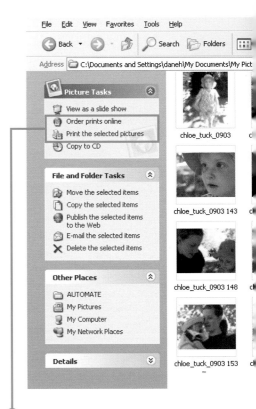

When browsing images in Windows XP, you can print quickly by using the common tasks bar located to the left of the window. These common tasks dynamically update based on the type of media you select.

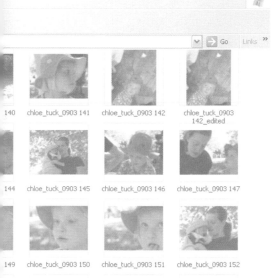

140   chloe_tuck_0903 141   chloe_tuck_0903 142   chloe_tuck_0903 142_edited

144   chloe_tuck_0903 145   chloe_tuck_0903 146   chloe_tuck_0903 147

149   chloe_tuck_0903 150   chloe_tuck_0903 151   chloe_tuck_0903 152

154   chloe_tuck_0903 155   chloe_tuck_0903 156   chloe_tuck_0903 157

Making Prints Work
Home and Online Printing Using Windows XP

The convenience of personal printing has come a long way. The quality you can produce in the home today was only available professionally just a few years ago. Whether you create personal projects or scrapbooks, the cost, convenience, and quality of your prints rely on a few important items:

> **Resolution.** This is true for both the camera *and* the printer. The higher the resolution, the better chance for a crisp, clear image. With digital cameras, this is measured in megapixels. With printers, this is measured in DPI (dots per inch).

> **Software.** Print wizards and auto templates make it easy to print onto standard size papers and give you an option to preview before you print.

> **Paper.** The quality and finish of the paper will have a profound affect on the quality and finish of the print. Before you buy (or use) a printer, evaluate the paper quality and cost to print. You might find that your investment is spent equally on the printer and the paper.

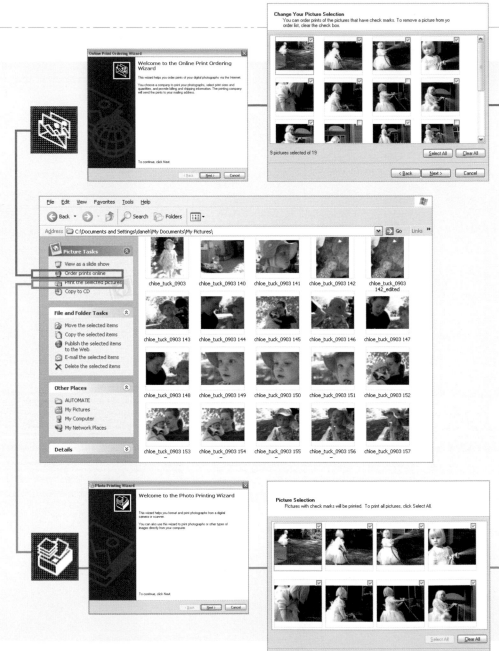

Select a Printing Company
The companies below print high-quality photographs.

Select a company to print your photographs.
Companies:

- Print@FUJICOLOR
  With MSN Photos, you can order FUJIFILM prints of your favorite pictures
- Shutterfly
  Get high quality prints and more from your digital pictures.
- Kodak print services by Ofoto®
  Order Kodak-quality prints of all your digital pictures; delivered worldwide.

< Back   Next >   Cancel

MSN® Photos
Select the pictures, print sizes, and quantity you want to print.

Select a size and quantity for all images:

4" x 6" [1] [v]   5" x 7" [ ] [v]   8" x 10" [ ] [v]

| | 8" x 10" | | $3.29 |

Help

Quantity	Print Size	Unit Price	Price
1	4" x 6"	$0.49	$0.49
	5" x 7"	$1.29	
	8" x 10"	$3.29	

Quantity	Print Size	Unit Price	Price
1	4" x 6"	$0.49	$0.49
	5" x 7"	$1.29	

$4.41 subtotal + $1.95 shipping = $6.36

< Back   Next >   Ca

Connect to photosopw.msn.com

Please sign in with your .NET
Passport to use all of the great
features on MSN Photos.

E-mail address: [ ]
Password: [••••••••••••]
☐ Sign me in automatically

OK   Cancel

Get a .NET Passport   Help

.net

Secure account information is an important part of the online print solution.

SELECT A PRINTER: ONLINE

Online printing companies (shown above) provide secure online services where you can upload and edit your images. Three such companies are shown here.

SELECT A PRINTER: HOME

For home and network printing (shown below), printer selection is designated to a specific piece of hardware.

SIZE, LAYOUT, AND QUANTITY

A customized display gives you the ability to choose the layout, size, and quantity of the images you'd like to print. In the online example (above), price is also totaled.

For home printing (below), layout and page size is shown in the preview. In both examples, 4 × 6 prints are the desired size.

PROFESSIONAL ONLINE

The quality and finish of online prints are identical to the professional prints at any film-based developer. The photos are usually shipped directly to your home. Orders can be easily duplicated and sent to multiple households for quick distribution and sharing across many people.

It's a great feeling to get pictures in the mail.

Printing Options
Select the printer and paper you want to use.

What printer do you want to use?
[ ] [v]   Install Printer...

Your prints will look best if you select the correct paper before printing. To select paper, click Printing Preferences.

Printing Preferences

< Back   Next >   Cancel

Layout Selection
Select a layout from the choices below.

Available layouts:

cropped and rotated to fit

4 x 6 in. Prints

4 x 6 in. cutout prints:
cropped and rotated to fit

4 x 6 in. album prints:
cropped to fit

Number of times to use each picture: [1]

Print preview:

< Back   Next >   Cancel

CONVENIENT HOME/OFFICE

Immediate and tangible prints are the primary benefits of home office printing. The print quality relies on the printer and paper. A greater degree of control over layout adds increased flexibility to personal projects.

Creating a collage in seconds is fantastic.

Custom Prints and Collage

Using Microsoft Picture It! Digital
Image Suite 9

I discovered a way to create prints and collages *very* quickly. The process was so quick
that I have adopted it for digital output as well.
The process illustrated to the right was used
a number of times to create spreads and art-
work for this book. This process begins in
Microsoft Digital Image Library.

1. Select the images you want in your collage
   by pressing and holding the CTRL key while
   selecting the thumbnails.

2. Right-click to bring up the menu and select
   Print. Digital Image Pro 9 will automatically
   open.

3. Follow the steps in Print Layout menu.

4. Edit and compose the layout by clicking and
   dragging within the picture boxes (steps 5
   through 6). Select your cropping options.

5. Select the quantity of desired prints.

6. Check the box to keep a digital copy of the
   collage template. This will give you flexibility
   to edit and share it digtitally if you wish.

I think the most remarkable aspect of this tip
is that it empowers you to contextually select
and edit a compostion *very* quickly. Additonally,
if you share your images via hard copy or soft
copy, this process becomes a quick and easy
way to author.

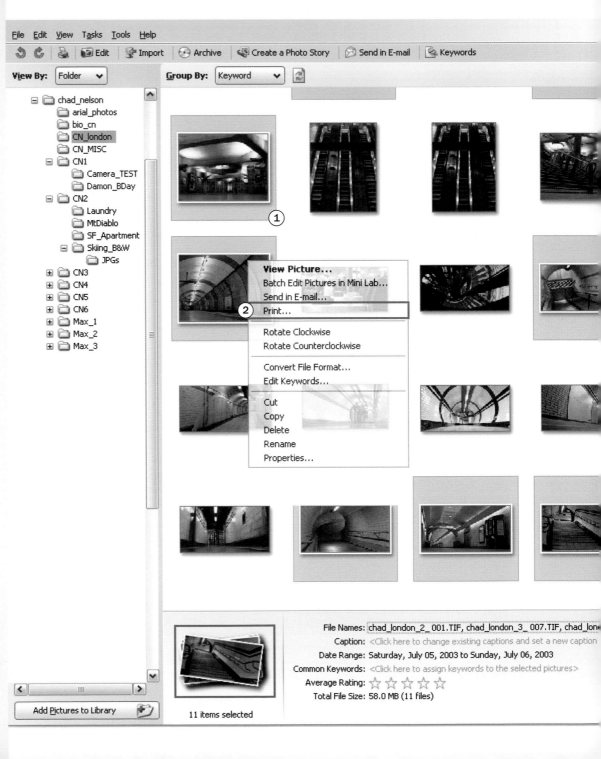

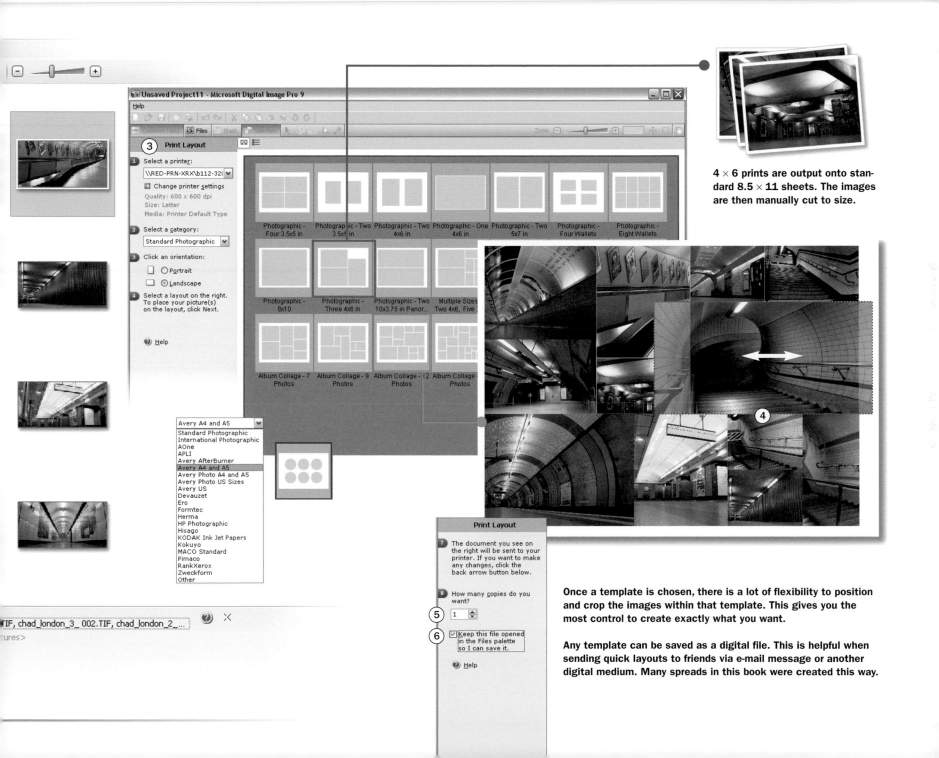

4 × 6 prints are output onto standard 8.5 × 11 sheets. The images are then manually cut to size.

Once a template is chosen, there is a lot of flexibility to position and crop the images within that template. This gives you the most control to create exactly what you want.

Any template can be saved as a digital file. This is helpful when sending quick layouts to friends via e-mail message or another digital medium. Many spreads in this book were created this way.

A Quick Guide to Sharing
Using Adobe Photoshop Album 2.0

The Quick Guide in Photoshop Album 2.0 is a great launch pad for sharing your photos. The icons in the guide provide a simple way to jump into a desired format. Upon selecting the icon, a simple interface guides you through the options necessary for output.

The great thing I have noticed is that this program is built for speed. I was able to select images and print and e-mail them very quickly. This is a great tool for sharing different types of media with multiple people.

(1) Multiple images can be selected from the photo well by holding down the CTRL key while selecting with your mouse.

(2) The Quick Guide (Help, QuickGuide) can be used to quickly access tasks that are used often.

(3) Hard copies can be made either by printing locally or by ordering professional prints online.

(4) Soft copy e-mail messages can be quickly authored by attaching your images and controlling the size.

(5) This ability to control image size is very helpful when sending to those with slower connections.

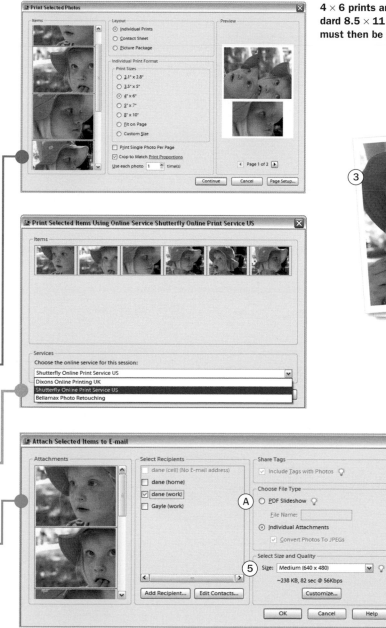

4 × 6 prints are output onto standard 8.5 × 11 sheets. The images must then be manually cut to size.

123 address way
anywhere, USA

Online photo ordering usually comes with a contact sheet for reference. Prints are sent via postal mail based on your preferences and size requests.

An e-mail attachment allows you to author and attach images quickly and easily. In the view shown here, the file size is represented in each attached file. For a sequential (and single file) option, choose a PDF attachment. Ⓐ This option will attach a single file rather than a number of smaller image files.

Books Made Easier...
Using Adobe Photoshop Album 2.0 and MyPublisher

If you had asked me to create a book, I would have frozen like a deer in headlights. If you had asked me to select a bunch of my favorite photos and explain what they were about, the task would have been less daunting.

The process to select and output your images into a book format is becoming increasingly easier, especially using user-friendly software that is designed to guide you through the process. I had the privilege of trying this software a couple times, and the quality was amazing. I kept coming back...

① From Adobe Photoshop Album, access the Creations Wizard and select the Photo Book from the list of creations.

② Using the Creations Wizard, follow the easy steps (2 through 6) that allow you to quickly design your own photo books based on the available templates.

NOTE: For more advanced control over your bookmaking, visit **www.mypublisher.com** and download the custom bookmaking software.

For more information, visit **www.futureofmemories.com**.

The Creations Wizard gives you access to multiple projects quickly. The setup and selection process is mainly the same. If you're looking for more flexibility in your templates, visit the Adobe website and inquire about downloading additional templates.

② A series of template styles allow you to choose the presentation style and layout of your book.

③ The book setup will define the context and propogate through-out the pages. The title can be the single most important con-text for the pages that follow.

④ Photo selection and ordering will be a primary interface for grouping and editing within the template you have chosen. ⑤ This will show you how your pages will look and how to order your story. You might want to create multiple versions quickly to compare and contrast before you commit to output. Be sure you ad-just the cropping and positioning as well.

Publish Your Photo Book
Step: 1 2 3 4 5 ⑥

⑥

Publishing your pages is getting easier and easier. In the example above, you can publish directly using a professional print company. Using a se-cure account, you can have your books automatically mailed anywhere in the world.

The New Film

I don't feel bad borrowing a camera anymore. Friends never send copies of pictures, anyway. I just bring my "film" with me and snap a few shots, removing my CF card when I am done. Portability and flexibility are the key.

I reached into my pocket the other day and pulled out some pocket change…and 150 photographs! I had just made a trip to the store and made some quick prints of a weekend trip we took with the kids. I realized the power of what I was carrying with me. My CF (compact flash) card had become more than photo storage. It was truly portable media.

I now carry one with me everywhere I go.

> **Take/show *your* prints.** I like this. You don't even really need a camera if you're out with friends. Sometimes I just bring the card. I'll ask to borrow their camera for a little bit to take some photos. They're a little cautious until they realize what I'm doing. I've even used their camera to show them shots I've taken. This tip gives you a lot of freedom. Have you ever asked to have friends send you prints? They rarely get around to it. Take your own pictures. Give yourself the chance to own them.

> **Get or copy a file (or two).** This isn't just for images. Use your media card to copy documents, media, or *any* type of file you'd like to copy. I learned this in Europe. I was traveling with a business colleague on a train. The presentation was in 20 minutes, and he had the entire presentation on his laptop. He blew me away when he took the card out of his camera, copied the presentation to the card, and gave it to me to put onto my laptop. This changed my whole world. (The presentation went over really well.)

For more information on portable memory, see www.futureofmemories.com.

Take a CF card to the photo lab.

Where you take your film today is where you will begin to take your media cards. Ask your local retailer about their formats and prices. Urge them to get with it...soon.

Stick it in your printer.

If you're in the market for a printer, ask yourself if you want to print directly from your printer. Evaluate if this is an imporant feature when printing for yourself.

Show it on dad's TV.

You can use your camera's video cable to run a slide show or movie using Photo Story. Alternatively, more and more monitors and TVs are considering media card readers for display in the home.

Keep it on your phone.

My cell phone now has a camera. It came with a smart media card. I can send e-mail from my phone. I can take pictures and send them, instantly.

Give it to a friend.

It's just storage. Use it for photo and media sharing. It will hold any media type you choose to put on it. This is not your dad's floppy disk.

Run it through an X-ray machine.

Delight in the fact that your photos should be safer when traveling through the airport. No more pulling out the film and worrying that it will get exposed.

Move it around, a lot.

Buy a few and use them, relentlessly. Find ways to keep them with you, and delight in their flexibility and the ability to fill them up, again and again.

Sharing Over Time...

There is an emotional scale that is amplified by time and resolution when we share our images. The resolution of the image can effectively be lower when a memory is shared immediately (such as in mobile phone or e-mail messages). As time passes, that image takes on a different role. The longer the time period, the greater the need for resolution and context. The image ultimately can reach "memorial" status if it makes it into print or an album. As you begin to author and share your images, diversify between mediums and across time, allowing your audience to enjoy a full spectrum of experiences. A great way to manage this is to centralize your media using a digital image library.

"Thanks for thinking of me! Looks like you guys are having a great time."

"These pictures are great! I can't wait to hear more about your trip."

"It's so great to see the whole trip. The kids are so much bigger than they were last year at this time."

(approximate time until shared)

(30 seconds later)

(1–3 days later)

(1 day–1 month later)

● **Event occurs**

small size

medium size

medium size

(320 px × 240 px)
(640 px × 480 px)

(640 px × 480 px)
(800 px × 600 px)
(1024 px × 768 px)
on up...

(640 px × 480 px)
(800 px × 600 px)
(1024 px × 768 px)
on up...

Digital camera on phone; e-mail or multi-media message sent via mobile phone.

Photos transferred to computer and e-mailed to friends or family.

Photos prepared and posted on a website gallery.

A single image can be shared for years.

Different mediums provoke different kinds of responses. Some communicate immediacy, whereas others memorialize the events that they portray. As you develop your living library, don't invest too heavily in one technology or medium. Give yourself the flexibility to share in many mediums.

HIGH-RESOLUTION

Lasting memories usually take more time and care to author. The fidelity of the story can be rich with detail, but lasting memories take the most time and effort to produce. Better software is changing this. You can now author and print your memories within hours of them occuring.

"Thanks for sending the prints! I've put some of my favorites in frames and some others on the fridge."

"Thanks for showing this to me. This is a great record of all your trips. You're going to cherish this when they are older."

"This is an amazing body of work."

(days–months later)

(months–years later)

large size

(1024 px × 768 px)
2 megapixel
3 megapixel
on up...

largest size

3 megapixel
4 megapixel
on up...

Professional photos printed and sent via mail.

Printed books and albums.

Sharing Soft Copies...

The most prolific area of photo sharing is in soft copy distribution. Increasing numbers of devices and display technologies coupled with Internet growth have enabled a multitude of authoring and viewing opportunities ranging from cell phones to TVs.

One of the most important aspects of soft copy sharing is understanding the presentation capabilities across mediums. Soft copies range from fully interactive experiences to linear slide shows and documents. Richer experiences combine audio and music coupled with animation and rich typography. Some emulate those of a home movie experience or DVD.

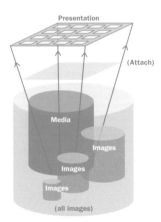

👁 **E-mail is still one of the most widely used and accessible ways to send soft copies of images, yet very few people know how to send and optimize a cohesive and effective experience.**

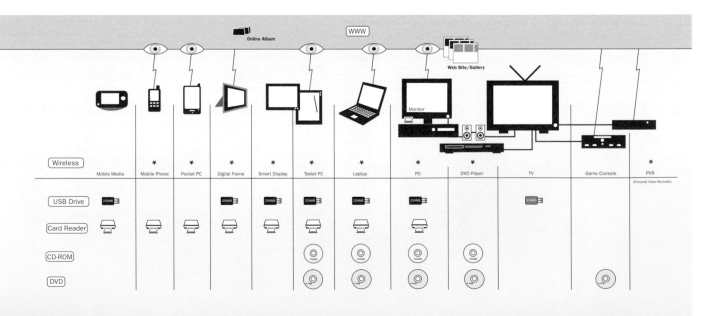

People & Chat   Encarta   Photos

Some attachments, such as a PDF or WMV (Windows Media Video) format movie file, make the viewing experience better for the recipient. Each of these formats has the ability to uniquely control the viewing experience.

Using the Inserting Pictures feature will give you greater flexibility when authoring and sending e-mail messages. Use the Attach File feature when sending file types other than images.

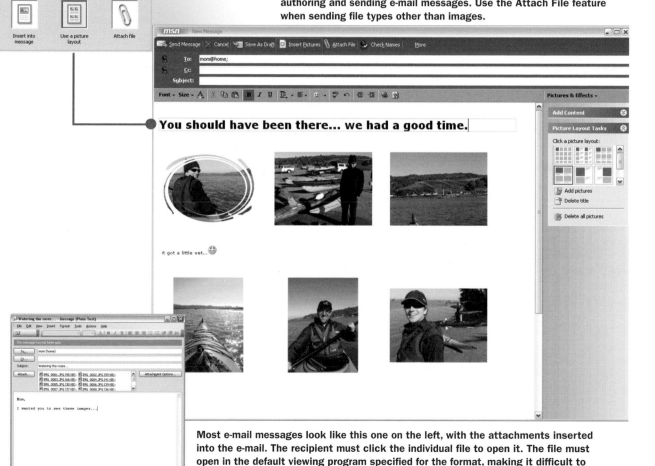

Most e-mail messages look like this one on the left, with the attachments inserted into the e-mail. The recipient must click the individual file to open it. The file must open in the default viewing program specified for the format, making it difficult to see all images at the same time.

Effective E-Mail

HTML E-MAIL...
is formatted to display within the page, allowing the page to be formatted. These pages look much better when they are shared.

A DIGITAL PACKAGE...

Attaching a PDF file to an e-mail message allows you to carefully control the presentation of your images. In this format, all your images can be included into a single file. They can even include audio.

A PHOTO STORY...
is formatted as a movie by Microsoft Plus! Photo Story and can be attached as a single file. When opened, the movie presents a rich experience with animation and sound.

Slide Shows

It used to be that a slide show was merely the presentation of one static image after another. This is beginning to change. A slide show can contain many images that are driven by a template language. The presentation itself can be updated to accomodate different viewing experiences on a variety of platforms. The image order and timing can be changed independently from the images themselves. A single slide show can be output to view on a Pocket PC or on a widescreen television. The beauty of the sequential imagery is that the presentations themselves take on a rich quality where the presentation of the images themselves become the backbone for how the story is received. In a way, think of a slide show as a movie in slow motion.

As mentioned in Section 1, slide shows and image presentations are great using Microsoft Plus! Photo Story. The primary emphasis should be on choosing the right images and putting them in the right order.

In this example, Adobe Photoshop Album is used to create a slide show. First a series of image thumbnails is selected. The Create button is selected to open the Creation Wizard.

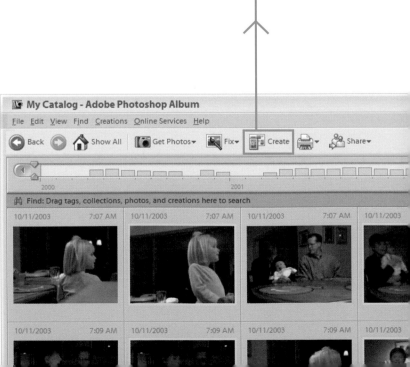

Set up Your Slideshow

Step: 1 2 3 4 5 6

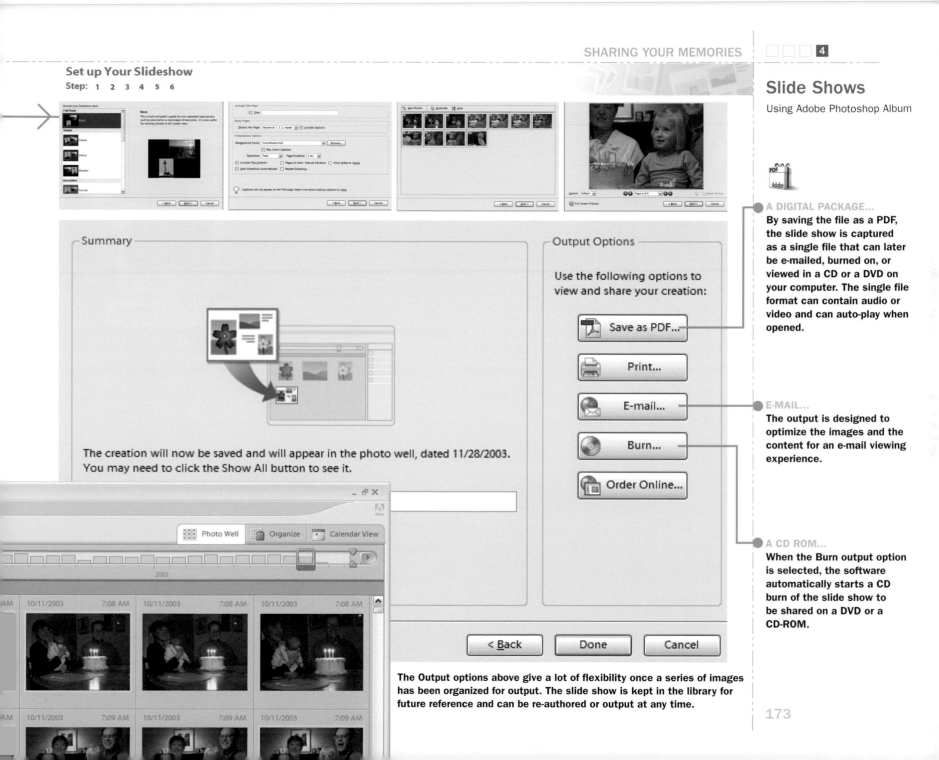

Slide Shows

Using Adobe Photoshop Album

A DIGITAL PACKAGE...

By saving the file as a PDF, the slide show is captured as a single file that can later be e-mailed, burned on, or viewed in a CD or a DVD on your computer. The single file format can contain audio or video and can auto-play when opened.

Summary

The creation will now be saved and will appear in the photo well, dated 11/28/2003. You may need to click the Show All button to see it.

Photo Well   Organize   Calendar View

2003

10/11/2003	7:08 AM	10/11/2003	7:08 AM	10/11/2003	7:08 AM
10/11/2003	7:09 AM	10/11/2003	7:09 AM	10/11/2003	7:09 AM

Output Options

Use the following options to view and share your creation:

- Save as PDF...
- Print...
- E-mail...
- Burn...
- Order Online...

E-MAIL...

The output is designed to optimize the images and the content for an e-mail viewing experience.

A CD ROM...

When the Burn output option is selected, the software automatically starts a CD burn of the slide show to be shared on a DVD or a CD-ROM.

< Back   Done   Cancel

The Output options above give a lot of flexibility once a series of images has been organized for output. The slide show is kept in the library for future reference and can be re-authored or output at any time.

173

Slide Shows (continued)
Immersive Experiences

A key benefit to a slide show or movie presentation is the ability to provide a more immersive experience. Often this benefit is overlooked. Some of the most compelling presentations borrow from formats that are inherent in TV and film. By presenting the content full frame, the viewing experience is controlled entirely by the author. Slide shows and dynamic media can produce some of the most compelling experiences on a computer or TV simply by presenting the media full frame. The viewing experience is enhanced by:

> **Viewing Full Screen.** Content presentations that fill the screen with an image reduce clutter and fill the display with a full experience.

> **Sequential Stills.** This is "poor man's" video, but can be very compelling. When video and sound are not available, sequential stills provide context and sequence to a series of imagery when presented together.

> **Simple Transitions.** There are only a few transitions that are worth talking about. A simple cross-disolve or pan-fade are subtle and effective. Transitions are best when they do not distract from the content. They should also perform well on the platform they are presented on.

> **Simple Typography.** If a caption is a part of the presentation, keep the typography simple and easy to read.

> **Audio.** Sound is an easy way to create mood and context. This is often overlooked or misused. Choose your audio carefully. It can make or break a presentation.

Media presentations that play the content full screen are easy to author and share. In Windows XP a slide show can be created easily by clicking on the Slide Show icon or by pressing F11, shown below. In Microsoft Digital Image Library (at right), a slideshow can be viewed by double-clicking the thumbnail.

Start Slide Show (F11)

The slide show viewer in Microsoft Digital Image Library combines smooth transitions with timing controls. A key distinction between slideshow viewers is how they handle transitions between images.

www.chadandkeek.com

Chad & Keek's
London Holiday
2003

An index can provide a compelling invitation into an immersive experience. Explanations are key to thread a story together.

A room for any mood.

A rainbow of illumination options. Just turn the dial on the lightswitch...and you'll go from cool to vibrant red.

St. Martins Lane Hotel.

Ian Schragger is known for his ultra-hip hotels...and St. Martins Lane, designed by Philippe Starck, is no exception. Let's take a quick tour...

Covent Garden.

What better way to explore the streets of London than in a bright orange convertible VW Bug? We hopped from one boutique to the next.

The London Eye.

Built for the millennium celebration, the Eye offers incredible views of the Thames and beyond. And with the skies so blue...we couldn't pass it up.

Camden Town.

This was my first time back in over a decade. We had fun exploring their famous Sunday morning outdoor markets.

The Tate Modern.

We saw the largest-ever inflatable sculpture—entitled "Blockhead." An afternoon from one of the reading rooms.

London Underground.

A delightful bit of photography set in the tunnels of the London subway.

4

MOVIES AND MEDIA

With Plus! Photo Story, a simple wizard-like interface is used to create linear movies and media.

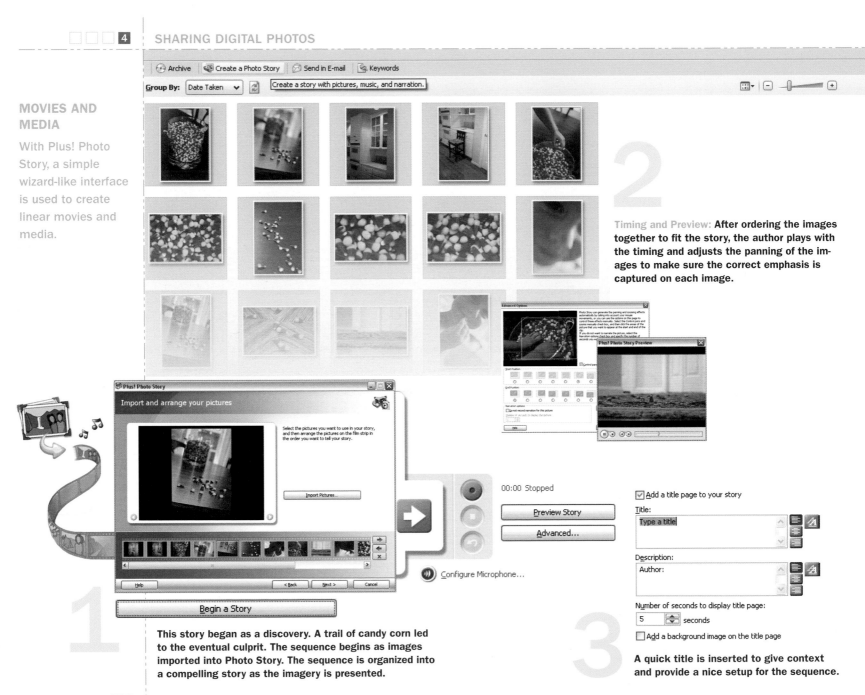

Archive | Create a Photo Story | Send in E-mail | Keywords

Group By: Date Taken | Create a story with pictures, music, and narration.

Timing and Preview: After ordering the images together to fit the story, the author plays with the timing and adjusts the panning of the images to make sure the correct emphasis is captured on each image.

Plus! Photo Story

Import and arrange your pictures

Select the pictures you want to use in your story, and then arrange the pictures on the film strip in the order you want to tell your story.

Import Pictures...

Help | < Back | Next > | Cancel

Begin a Story

This story began as a discovery. A trail of candy corn led to the eventual culprit. The sequence begins as images imported into Photo Story. The sequence is organized into a compelling story as the imagery is presented.

00:00 Stopped

Preview Story

Advanced...

Configure Microphone...

☑ Add a title page to your story

Title:
Type a title

Description:
Author:

Number of seconds to display title page:
5 seconds

☐ Add a background image on the title page

A quick title is inserted to give context and provide a nice setup for the sequence.

I wanted to share the story in a way that captured how I had experienced it. Adding the music was easy, and it adds a lot to the final movie.

▶ Now Playing   ⌄ _ ☐ ✕

A trail of candy... corn

☐ Album Art

Ready

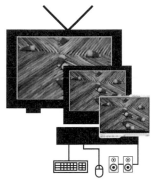

CHOOSE YOUR SIZE

A movie can be output with a specific viewing experience in mind. Photo Story allows for multiple sizes to acco- modate e-mail, web, or TV viewing.

4

Background music

☑ Add background music to your story.

Music file:

<music file>   Browse...

Background music volume:

Low   High

Preview Final Story

Ambiance and Final Preview: **A playful music file is added to enhance the discovery feeling that led to the missing candy corn.**

5

Output Final Story: **The final movie gives the story a polish and a professional quality, despite the fact that it was created quickly using simple tools.**

Video quality

◉ High quality (640x480 resolution provides better playback quality on your computer)

○ Medium quality (320x240 resolution uses a smaller file size)   Advanced...

Audio quality

◉ High quality (CD-quality audio provides a better playback experience on your computer)

○ Medium quality (FM-quality audio uses a smaller file size)

Save story

File name:

PhotoStory1.wmv   Browse...

Smarter Templates

*I needed
a flexible
template that
I could use
with a map
or a paper
napkin
sketch.*

Some of the most exciting advances in media creation and authoring are happening in the design of media-driven templates. These are presentations that have a logic and a behavior built into the presentation layer. They range greatly in quality and performance, but they are beginning to take on fluid animation and dynamic behaviors. The interfaces that began as experiments by designers and programmers are beginning to find a voice in major applications. Some can be customized to fit your own needs, while others are built as library extensions off of major applications.

Smart Templates are used in interactive media, web applications, and DVD authoring.

*I like dynamic templates a lot more than slide
shows. They give me a freedom to explore the
media on my own terms and at my own pace.
They provide a sense of discovery.*

The images above are driven by the same template. Designed by Eric Rodenbeck, the behavior of the template has a few subtle nuances about it that make the experience unique each time it is viewed. For more information about smart templates, visit www.futureofmemories.com.

MAPS AND LOCATION

This two panel presentation uses a location-specific index on the right to target a specific image on the left. This template uses spatial relationships to help provide context, giving the user a sense of place and context.

DYNAMIC SEQUENCE

This presentation uses sequential stills to suggest context and order. The images scroll in from right to left, allowing the viewer to easily advance through the material.

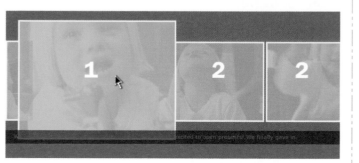

MULTI-PANEL

This is a four-quadrant presentation that enlarges the image when it is selected. The caption is always presented in the center. This type of presentation may imply sequence, but uses multiple images to show continuity.

Dynamic Media Creation
Using iZotope PhotonShow

Every once and a while an application comes along that has all the right thinking presented in an easy-to-digest interface. When I first saw iZotope PhotonShow, I immediately recognized that it used Macromedia Flash. The more I looked into it, the more I realized that it was a sophisticated application with an extensible template language.

One of the key benefits of PhotonShow is the ability to author and extend the templated themes. Anyone using Macromedia Flash can create templates using the tool.

As an exercise in media authoring and presentation, I teamed up with some of my talented contributors to present a customized set of templates designed to be used with PhotonShow. The dynamic media presentations created for this book were designed as experiments in interaction. To learn more, visit:

www.futureofmemories.com/templates
www.photonshow/memories

I use the tool to quickly export .swf files that I use on my website and e-mail to friends. They always ask me to send more...

WIZARD-LIKE AUTHORING
PhotonShow allows you to author numerous projects while changing the template quickly. The themes (at right) that were designed specifically for this book take advantage of dynamic animation and text display. Each template is designed to look and behave differently.

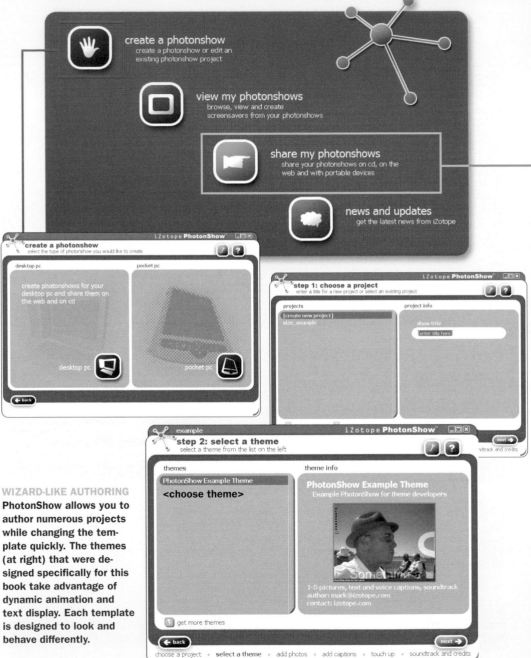

share on web   burn to cd   transfer to pocket pc

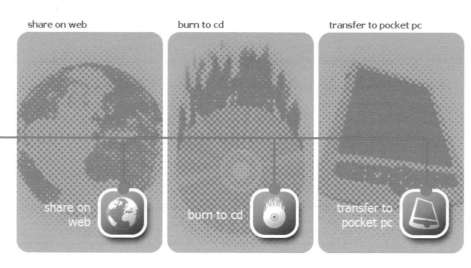

share on web

burn to cd

transfer to pocket pc

EASY SHARING

The PhotonShow wizard allows you to quickly output a presentation that is optimized for the web, CD, or a mobile device. PhotonShow automatically adjusts the image size and output to be optimized for each.

FINAL OUTPUT

Each PhotonShow is output in a single file format (.swf) that contains all of the optimized images, captions, and audio. You can output your stories anywhere on your local drive by adjusting the settings (indicated by the blue wrench icon.)

step 3: add photos
select a folder, select photos, and click 'add selected' to copy them to the filmstrip

My Downloads
My eBooks
My Music
My Pictures
 _month_day_
 Ad
 AUTOMATE
  test _upload
  test
 BACKUP
 _upload
 contributors

step 4: add captions
add text and voice captions to each photo in the filmstrip

text caption
[enter caption here]
<write caption>

voice caption
set voice caption

step 5: touch up
use the photo processing tools to touch up each photo in the filmstrip

remove redeye   rotate
trim and crop   flip
adjust lighting
adjust color   reset photo
sharpen
soft focus
remove dust and speckles

step 6: soundtrack and credits
choose a soundtrack, enter credits, and click 'next' to save your photonshow

soundtrack
soundtrack filename
<choose soundtrack>
soundtrack preview
play   volume control

credits
author
Dane
date
Jan 1st, 2004
credits
[enter credits here]

CUSTOMIZATION MADE EASY

Steps 4 through 6 give you added flexibility to add captions to each image as well as touch up specific qualities of the image itself. The application handles all of the treatments independent from the original, so you do not have to worry about altering your original. In step 6, an audio soundtrack can be added to enhance the presentation.

Memory sharing and browsing can be done in the living room by remote control. By using the Microsoft Windows XP Media Center Edition, images can be centralized and showcased in the room where your media is best suited. For more information visit: www.microsoft.com/mediacenter.

Movies, Media, and **Beyond**

Memory sharing is no stranger to the living room. At center stage of your home theater is most likely a VCR, a DVD player, and a TV. There might be a computer there very soon, masked in a box that looks nothing like a computer as you know it today. These new media computers are becoming a central hub for media viewing, recording, and browsing. Some prominent features might include:

> **The Personal Video Recorder (PVR).** This device allows you to record and playback TV and other media that you've recorded, allowing you to control your TV viewing experience. Some digital library software can output directly to a PVR format.

> **DVD/CD Player.** This device allows you to play DVD movies, CDs, and MP3 files. This is probably the most ubiquitous digital player found in the living room to showcase and share your images. It requires DVD burning capabilities on your computer.

> **Media Port.** An increasingly important feature for media connection, storage, and playback. Many digital cameras allow for video playback already, but some include a media port to directly accept a media card or digital connection.

This conceptual prototype was designed as a docking bay for a number of devices.

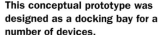

DEMYSTIFY:
DVD-ROM, DVD-R,
DVD-RAM, DVD-RW,
DVD+RW

DVD authoring is a quick way to get your presentations into the living room; however there are a number of DVD formats to keep track of. For a quick reference, go to the web and search on "DVD Formats" for the latest in DVD authoring software and format comparisons.

The Windows Powered Smart Display is a touch-sensitive screen that wirelessly communicates with your home PC, allowing you to freely interact or display any media you wish.

Smarter Displays

As devices become smaller and more connected, so will their presentations. An example of this is showing up in digital picture frames, photo receivers, and smart displays. The biggest advantage of these display surfaces is their ability to operate intelligently without being tethered to a computer. Many of the smarter devices use wireless technology or a simple modem to transparently connect to a connected Internet source to access images and other media. The first wave of these products is available now. Many will be controlled by the home PC or media PC. Smart displays access the images automatically. This is critical for how you begin to think about sharing your images, albums, and presentations.

Instead of authoring and sending your presentations, you'll manage a "playlist," much like you manage your digital music. This allows you to set up dynamic and personalized viewing experiences specific to time and location.

"I have a new favorite routine. Every morning I sit down in my kitchen with a cup of coffee and my grandchildren."

My mom, Diane Howard

The images stored locally on your computer can be uploaded to a secure online account, where multiple smart frames can download and display images. Recipients can choose to print those images they like.

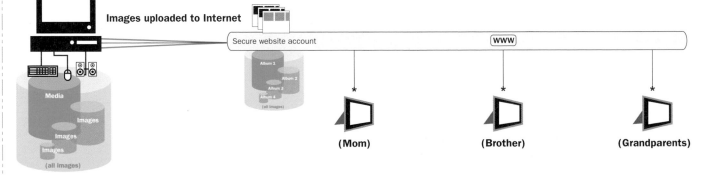

Images uploaded to Internet

Secure website account   WWW

(Mom)   (Brother)   (Grandparents)

The Ceiva Digital Photo Receiver is one example of a smart picture frame. It is designed to automatically display a digital slide show and can be placed anywhere in the home. Each night, the receiver makes a local call to the Internet to receive pictures that have been sent to it from anywhere in the world. For more information, visit www.ceiva.com.

Increasingly **Mobile Memories**

Taking Pictures

Digital cameras are quietly sneaking onto mobile phones. With increasing memory and higher clarity, your mobile phone will play an increasingly important role in your image taking. You'll never have an excuse not to have your camera with you again if you have your camera phone close at hand. Your phone might be the most socially connected device you own.

Your reach is extended by Multimedia Messaging (MMS) and e-mail capabilities built right into the phone. Many phones already allow you to be on a phone call while you take a picture and send it to a friend. Smart contact lists can also keep the people you call most close, allowing you to manage and send images to multiple people at once. A camera phone isn't for everyone, however. Whether your phone becomes an increasingly better camera or your camera becomes increasingly connected, your mobility and flexibility will enable you to share your images with more expediency than ever before.

Taking Them with You

A great way to share your images is to take them with you. This is an exciting area with increasingly more choices. Mobile memory taking (cell phones and digital cameras) and mobile memory sharing (such as Portable Media Center, MP3 players, and USB keychains) are at the heart of mobile media. Your phone and your keychain are prime areas that will increase in memory and reduce in size and price.

A portable USB drive like the ones shown above can reach gigabyte sizes and more, and they can be attached to a keychain. Some models can accomodate media cards and aid in image transferring. For more information, go to www.usbdrives.com.

Integrated cameras are a key feature on the new mobile phones. Don't make the mistake of getting the camera as an accessory or an add-on. Make sure it is integrated.

sort by name ▸

▶ play slideshow

Montery Historic Races
9/12/02

Skylars 1st Birthday
10/21/02

Oregon Coast
7/28/03

Mud Lake
6/05/03

Cali Road Trip
5/12/02

PORTABLE MEDIA CENTER

The portability of your images will coincide with other media needs such as music, video, and TV. Quick and easy connections will make transferring, viewing, and sharing your media easy across the Media Center PC and a TV.

This early conceptual design illustrates the portability and size of the Portable Media Center.

189

Chapter Review

Effectively...

Sharing. These are the gifts that will last longer than yourself. As you prepare and share across your network of family and friends, build habits that allow you to build on each relationship you craft. Expect that each chapter in this experience will be a reflection of your documentation process and an invitation to bring those stories to life. This is your life, and it's worth sharing and remembering...time and time again.

"Everybody needs his memories. They keep the wolf of insignificance from the door."

Saul Bellow

Sharing Checklist

☐ Decide that sharing should be fun. If it's not, make changes.

☐ Find opportunities in your own share map.

☐ Diversify between convenient and professional prints. Set up a schedule to share regularly.

☐ Experiment with making a book. That will force you to make important decisions and commemorate those memories that you care about most.

☐ Make room for portable media. Carry it with you.

☐ Focus on authoring immersive experiences.

☐ Don't forget the importance of sound.

☐ Experiment with more effective e-mail messages. Send a digital package (or two).

☐ Imagine your home entertainment system... but with sharing capabilities. Make this an important criteria for your next purchase.

afterword
Your Own Legacy

"Memory…is the diary that we all carry about with us."

—Oscar Wilde

Strength Is in the Sharing…

We thrive by telling our stories, and by listening to others.

The world is getting closer, but it is also narrowly out of focus.

We have an increasing capacity to build and maintain relationships, yet our time to nurture them is decreasing. The act of sharing is both a personal and a behavioral choice. The courage to share is built on the knowledge of how to share, combined with the passion and incentive to do so.

Be happy…
　Create independence…
　　Build lasting impressions…
　　　Find and know love…
　　　　Build a body of work…
　　　　　Invest wisely…
　　　　　　Be remembered…

People can invest their entire lives building toward goals that represent a life of legacy. We long to be noticed, differentiated, and happy. Rarely do we have control over such things. Our memories represent those stories that are completely our own. They grow and prosper with retelling, and they enrich our lives. They are also ours for the taking, and ours for the making.

We have never been so empowered. We live in a new world of choice and sharing. Our boundaries are extended yet need to be increasingly private and secure. We author in one medium and consume in another.

A legacy begins with a memory and is expressed by emotions. It must be both a monument and a network. It should solicit the untold stories, enriched by the people who have come in contact with it.

Consider yourself a primary audience. Regardless of the size of your family or the network of friends, chances are that *you* will benefit most from these stories as they build over time.

Your audience will become the fuel behind your community and the natural resource for your memories. Even though your focal point might be personal, your audience will bring meaning, insight, and perspective to those experiences when shared.

Your memories are personal journeys and expressions of how you see and document what you care about. Those expressions can be realized only by you.

Your Lifelong Event

In this day of automatic cameras, it's the "automatic" part that can get us in trouble. On average, we spend less time thinking about the emotional effect of the image, and we spend too much time on optical quality and clarity. Images that convey feeling come from the heart, not technology. You don't have to know everything that your camera can do, but you can manipulate a few things to make your images tell more compelling stories. If done effectively, you'll be able to see the results immediately.

Sharing a story brings people together. It can be simple or complex, funny or frightening. The hard truth is that our lives are not always cheerful, and things happen that we cannot control. As you prepare to share your stories, it is important to find a balance on how comfortable you feel telling your story.

I encourage you to take chances, but not at the expense of your comfort level or your exposure. Taking chances will help you grow and give your work a texture and a voice.

Sharing your stories is probably the most fun you will have. Its delivery has no rules and is something completely personal. The stories that you tell and the memories that you share become the foundation of the relationships that you foster and reference points for the future.

"You may delay, but time will not."
—Benjamin Franklin

"No memory is ever alone; it's at the end of a trail of memories, a dozen trails that each have their own associations."

Louis L'Amour

contributors

> Christian Anthony

> Don Barnett

> Eric Cheng

> Christian Colando

> Ammon Haggerty

> Sean Uberoi Kelly

> William Lamb

> Chad Nelson

> Damon Nelson

> Emily Palmgren

> Eric Rodenbeck

> WWMX Team

Photo credit: page 28

Christian Anthony

Christian Anthony is a designer, a filmmaker, an illustrator, and a photographer based in San Francisco.

Christian has put together a number of photo collections including Transit, a five-year retrospective of San Francisco graffiti.

His last project was a documentary about the art rock band Oxbow titled *Music for Adults*.

Photographers he greatly admires include Gary Winogrand, William Klein, Lars Tunbjork, William Eggelston, and Ed Ruscha.

Christian thinks wandering is a good thing.

His one piece of advice is always have your camera with you. Always.

He thanks Niko, Eugene, Greg, Dan, and Manuel for their permission. And Dakota.

Christian Anthony: **www.3580.com**
Transit: **www.3580.com/transit**
Music for Adults: **www.theoxbow.com/musicforadults**
Oxbow: **www.theoxbow.com**
Manuel: **www.splatterpromotion.com**

Don Barnett

Don Barnett studied at Art Center College of Design in Pasadena, California, majoring in illustration/fine art.

His art is extremely varied with multidisciplined art styles, mixing ink washes, gouache, alkyds and oils, and sometimes watercolor and photography. There is a healthy infusion of digital mediums as well. He shows his work primarily in southern California.

So much of what Don has created over the years is in response to individual inspiration, almost always requiring the learning of a new discipline. The theme of icons made of both natural phenomena and creatures great and small recurs often in his work. Many works try to express the idea that science and spirit are of the same material and location. Many are more playful than that, but retain a surreal spirit.

Artist Quote

I am fascinated with the ways of the physical world. Harmony and compositional rhythm play major roles in my work. Special attention is given for those who live in the sea or under the ground, or those who can fly.

Reviews

"Technology and the Natural Spirit," *Artscene*, The Monthly Guide to Art in Southern California
    California, December 1993

"Un createur proche de l'univers enfantin," *l'Ordinateur Individuel*
    France, October 2000

"Circling the Light, transforming urban fantasies into spiritual visions"
    Desktop Publishers Journal

www.donbarnett.com

portrait of Don Barnett by Uncle Jerry

Photo credits: pages 91, 102, 103

Photo credits: pages 96, 97, 128, 129

Eric Cheng

Eric Cheng is a software engineer, a musician, and an underwater photographer with a propensity for thoroughly documenting his travels. Eric is known for his work in digital infrared photography and digital underwater photography, and has been featured in magazines such as *PDN*, *PEI*, *DIVE*, and *Shark Diver*, and numerous other publications, both print and online. He started experimenting with digital photography in early 1998, giving up film completely two years later.

His personal website is the culmination of years of chronicling his life online, featuring a daily web journal, informative articles about photography, more than twenty trip journals, and more than 10,000 photographs.

Eric is also the owner and editor of Wetpixel.com, a website dedicated to providing the latest information to the underwater digital photography community. Wetpixel features tutorials, reviews, galleries, and a community of more than 1000 underwater photographers, all united in the common desire to share both information and images.

To see more, go to:

Personal Website: **www.echeng.com**
Travel Journals: **www.echeng.com/travel**
Wetpixel.com: **www.wetpixel.com**

Christian Colando

A carton of post-dated Polaroid film and an SX-70 camera ignited Christian Colando's interest in image gathering. The instant gratification and abundance of these self-processing images helped to establish a method of working that he continues to pursue with digital equipment.

With a background as a designer, an illustrator, and a painter, Christian enjoys documenting both urban and natural environments and landscapes. The visible effects of time and the elements are a frequent source of inspiration, and he is regularly drawn to photograph surface textures, architectural form and detail, and especially the transitive qualities of sunlight.

Christian works as a designer at Microsoft and lives with his family in Seattle, Washington, where he spends as much time as he can with a camera in hand. A portfolio of his images may be viewed at:

www.colando.com/image_galleries

Photo credits: pages 18, 20, 56, 87, 88, 98, 99, 126, 127

Ammon Haggerty

Photo credits: pages
136–144, 146–149

Ammon Haggerty is a multidisciplinary designer/engineer living in the San Francisco Bay Area. Ammon comes from a computer science background and got his start developing multimedia applications. Through his exposure to multimedia and user interface design, he discovered the world of graphic arts, which has led to the study of graphic design, industrial design, and architecture.

Ammon was responsible for creating the design-centered personal play space Qaswa, a website created in 1995, which received many design awards and was published in several magazines and books. The website has since been updated, but the original site can still be accessed through **www.qaswa.com**.

Over the past three years, Ammon has developed technologies, methodologies, and theories relating to relational systems and collaborative content-sharing environments. An overview and progress of his work is documented on his website, **www.anaspace.com**.

Ammon is currently creating a multimedia broadband player application for Sawyer Media Systems (**www.sawyermedia.com**).

Other interests which distract him from completing his projects are photography, DJ'ing, restoration of an old ferry boat (**www.vallejo.to**), and furniture and lighting design.

Sean Uberoi Kelly
Research Software Developer
Social Computing Group, Microsoft Research

Sean Uberoi Kelly is a research software developer in the Social Computing Group at Microsoft Research (MSR), in Redmond, Washington. He is currently the lead developer for Wallop, a social/communications application for sharing personal media within social networks. He was previously a developer in MSR's Virtual Worlds Group, working on immersive content and authoring tools, audio, and multiuser interfaces. He graduated from Princeton University in 1992 with a B.A. in English literature and visual arts, afterwards working in architecture and design in New York City and then as a songwriter, a guitarist and a producer for Atlantic Records in Los Angeles, where he specialized in production on emergent digital audio systems. In 1995, he attended the University of Vermont, studying computer science, before he completed a Masters in Interactive Telecommunications at New York University's Tisch School of the Arts in 1998. Prior to coming to MSR, Sean worked extensively in immersive and projected real-time virtual environments with Jaron Lanier, as a web developer creating online university and educational community sites and user-generated knowledge databases, and in designing sensor-based interfaces to interactive displays. From 2000–2001, Sean was an adjunct professor at NYU/ITP, teaching a design and prototyping class entitled "The Multi-User Experience."

Photo credits: pages 214–216

http://mywallop.com

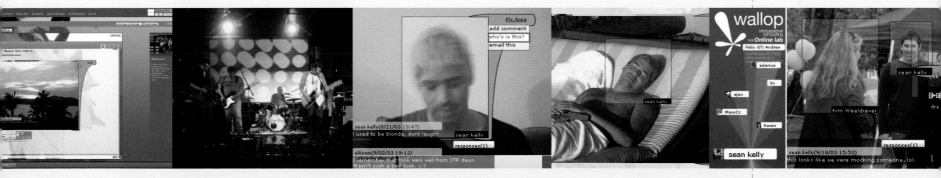

William Lamb

William Lamb is an attorney, a writer, and an aspiring photographer. He is a graduate of the University of Colorado at Boulder and the Northwestern School of Law at Lewis and Clark College. He has worked as a policy advisor for Senator Ted Kennedy, former Governor Romer of Colorado, and the Outdoor Recreation Coalition of America.

In 1997, William toured the country with the Lollapalooza music festival, working for the Surfrider Foundation by educating musicians and concertgoers on protecting the ocean, beaches, and waves. After a few years in the legal sector, he decided to pursue writing on a full-time basis. Currently, he is working on a series of socially conscious children's stories involving ferrets. Additionally, as a life-long film enthusiast, he recently founded a travel company geared towards taking film enthusiasts to the world's premier film festivals.

In his photography, William prefers the darker side of nature. His current work centers on the continuing loss of wilderness and the contamination of our natural world. He hopes to capture the Arctic National Wildlife Preserve in its pristine state before it is too late. Digital photography is his preferred medium because the photos feel alive and are easily transferable.

When not saving or traveling the world, William enjoys soccer, existentialist philosophy, and the *New York Times*. He resides in Boulder, Colorado.

Visit William at **www.flicktrips.com**.

Chad Nelson

Chad Nelson has been telling digital stories for more than a decade. With a background in fine art and theater, Chad spends his professional days conceptualizing, building, and evolving interactive media and entertainment for companies such as Sony Pictures, Microsoft, AOL Time Warner, and Virgin. However, that is simply his day job.

Whenever he finds a spare moment, Chad shares with the world the adventures of his son, Max, and wife, Allison, through his website **chadandkeek.com**. The site has redefined the family photo album and offers a source of inspiration for digital storytellers everywhere. Featuring everything from family hikes to karaoke-themed birthdays to reviews of retro sci-fi films, the site offers a bit of something for everyone. When Chad's son Max was born, his baby photos were viewed more than 17,000 times by nearly 1000 unique visitors. In the months that followed, the site grew to such a following that Sony caught wind of the website and now features it on their photography portal, Sony ImageStation. Chad created the site using Macromedia Flash MX to craft a series of "easy but flexible" templates. These templates allow him the ability to tailor each album to best capture the stories and images within.

Aside from family photos, Chad's portfolio includes series from his travels around the globe—with an emphasis on the diverse landscape of urban environments. Although he purchased his first digital camera in 1998, he found early digital cameras insufficient in terms of quality and features. When he made the switch to a 4 megapixel camera in 2001, however, digital quickly became his medium of choice (over 90% of his photos are now digital). When breaking this down into pure cost savings, Chad estimates that he now saves more than $3,000 per year by eliminating film and development costs. "I use film to capture singular moments," he states, "but with digital…I capture far more memories!" And for Chad, that makes all the difference.

www.chadandkeek.com
www.redthreds.com

Photo credits: pages 92, 93

Damon Nelson

Damon Nelson loves the photographic medium and has been shooting since he was very young. Inspired by the vibrant visuals of everyday life, he thinks of photography as an ideal way to capture beauty that is often over-looked. Damon currently lives and works in San Francisco, where he operates Clear For Launch, a design and photography studio. His professional work focuses on lifestyle, fashion, and product photography for various clients, including Sony and Red Threds Clothing. Artistically, Damon enjoys shooting vintage landscapes and relics in an attempt to capture places and details frozen in time amid the modern mania of urban sprawl.

Additional information and samples of work can be seen at **www.clearforlaunch.com**.

Emily Palmgren

Photo credits: pages 22, 23, 34, 100, 101, 178, 179

After working for more than a decade in the world of finance, Emily Palmgren walked away to be home full-time with her family: her first son (then a one-year-old), and her husband, Matt. "My career didn't fill me up, and I was finding that I couldn't do both well—be a mom and stockbroker at the level I was accustomed to. I think that if you absolutely love what you are doing, then it adds to your family's life, but if you don't, it takes everything out of you." Not knowing what career direction to head in, Matt, Emily, and their son (then two and a half years old) packed two backpacks and one umbrella stroller and headed for Italy for a month. By fate, a friend loaned Emily a Nikon N60. Emily dug in and started to learn how to use this new piece of equipment. That was it; she was more than hooked. "Never in a million years would I have thought I had such an artistic passion. Instantly, I started to see the world differently. Everything became a photograph, and when I looked through the lens, the world dropped away. I was frozen in that moment. Most surprising, I started to see people differently. Everyone I came across was beautiful and could be photographed in a unique and interesting way. People became my passion." Emily took on jobs quickly at cost to practice and expand her technique and eye. In the past year, she has photographed more than 300 unique faces. Her work is on display at Group Health Hospital Coop, and a handful of local stores, and she has been published in a national trade publication. She is currently working on a fun project, "scenes and flavors of Capitol Hill," for a Seattle gallery display. New adventures include a combination of painted canvas and photography, and most importantly their second son, born in October 2003.

Visit her website at **www.emilypalmgren.com** to view sample work. She can be reached at em@emilypalmgren.com for booking information.

Eric Rodenbeck

Eric Rodenbeck, creative director and founder of San Francisco–based Stamen Design, is one of the leading practitioners of template driven–design, a concept that's redefined the field of web design by enabling a flexible, graphically intensive, dynamic approach to web production.

In his role as Art and Narrative Director at Quokka.com, Eric helped spearhead the use of design templates to handle the enormous amounts of digital media submitted for the 2000 Sydney Olympics, the Whitbread Cup, and the assault on Great Trango Tower in Pakistan. The results were award-winning, visually breathtaking, and as close to the athletes' own experience as possible.

Recently Eric contributed the online, interactive templates that accompany this book, *Sharing Digital Photos*, a book that explores the way digital photography is changing how we think about our memories and the stories we tell about ourselves. These Flash templates enable newcomers to digital photography to assemble collections of their photographs, and then display and share their images in visually compelling slide shows and online albums.

Eric was born and raised in New York City, where he studied theoretical architecture at Cooper Union. After completing his degree in the history and philosophy of technology from the New School of Social Research, Rodenbeck moved to San Francisco in 1994. In addition to Quokka, Rodenbeck has worked at Umwow and Wired. His iconoclastic work has been featured in some of the most adventurous sites on the web, including Eye Magazine, The Remedi Project, K10K, The Codex Series, and Creative Review.

Stamen Design (**www.stamen.com**) was founded in 1997 to explore the intersection of graphics, interactive design, and online storytelling. Stamen Design has attracted a growing list of clients, including BMW, Macromedia, Moveon, and the San Francisco Museum of Modern Art.

WWMX Team
Ron Logan, Asta Roseway, and Kentaro Toyama

The World Wide Media eXchange (**www.wwmx.org**) project at Microsoft Research explores problems related to geographic location tags on digital imagery. The WWMX team consists of Ron Logan (software engineer), Asta Roseway (designer), and Kentaro Toyama (researcher).

Ron has worked for Microsoft since 1994 with product groups such as Visual C++, MSN, HomeAdvisor, and Tablet PC. He has a B.S. in literature from MIT and owns several copies of his favorite novel, *Moby Dick*. He is driving his wife insane by constantly toting multiple GPS devices around with him everywhere he goes.

Asta has been at Microsoft Research since 1997. Prior to that, she spent four years in Paris, where she earned her degree in graphic design from Parsons School of Design and ate lots of cheese. She helps run an annual tech camp for high school girls called "Digigirlz" and can be found fencing at the local salle. Asta reluctantly carried around a GPS device while working with the WWMX team but conveniently left it in her office when no one was looking.

Unlike Asta, Kentaro is unable to shake his inner nerd; he has carried a handheld GPS unit on his person for almost two years straight…and counting. Stalking and tracking of various kinds has been the focus of his professional career since graduate school. His dissertation, titled "Robust Vision-Based Object Tracking," was about computing object trajectories in live video.

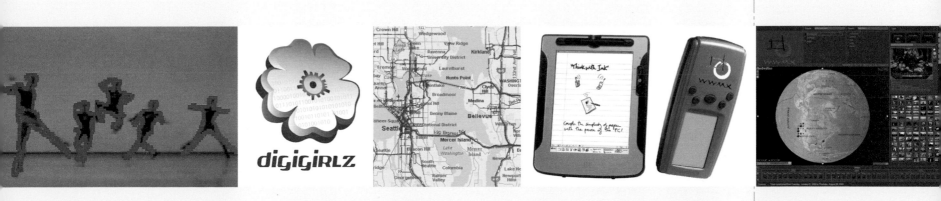

appendix

The Practice of Preparation

When you are building a virtual memory album, a little considera-
tion up front can make delivery go much more smoothly. What
follows are a few practices I have found useful. None of these
suggestions is necessary or required. I have included them as
helpful springboards to get you going. You will find that a commitment to one of them can spawn a few more ideas of your own.

Write a Mission Statement or a Dedication

Yes, a mission statement. This is part of your vision.
No, this doesn't have to be something that will define
the rest of your life. You don't even have to show it to
anyone. The idea is to get you writing. I wrote a small
dedication statement right before my daughter was born.
I'm really glad I did. What was special for me was that it
forced me to affirm all the reasons that I wanted to have
this child and how I was going to love her and her life.
I could have written it on a piece of paper, but I chose to
put it on the website. It soon became the foundation for
everything I was going to include and remember by creating this website for her.

A mission statement should be a statement of truth, and
it should provide direction. It usually contains the elements surrounding your values and keeps you on track
when you are in the middle a long project. A good mission statement will make your efforts timeless.

Set Up E-Mail

Set e-mail up for you and everyone else within your community network. It's worth it now to show them how to
use e-mail and how to set it up. Show them how they
can view attachments, and see if they can receive HTML
e-mail messages, which allow you to send images and
text in more controlled way.

Keep a Journal

This suggestion is a tough one, but it allows you to begin
to log and capture events and review them in your mind.
Keeping a journal does remarkable things for your ability
to craft and tell the stories later. If you can find a way to
journal regularly, it will be a great source of content and
reference later.

Set Up Instant Messaging

Instant messaging (IM) is like e-mail, but it uses a different technology. IM is sometimes called "chatting" on-line. Imagine a conference call every time you go online. Your computer detects who is online, and lets you know that you and some of your "buddies" are free to chat. You can all go into one area to chat, or you can have a dialogue one-on-one. Here, the text is sent to them immediately and seen on their screen immediately. It's faster than e-mail and has immediate gratification.

Set Up an Online Photo Account

Online photography services offer top-quality prints for digital and film camera users as well as traditional film processing. These services will provide private online image sharing and storing of multiple groups of photos that you upload. They are in business to help alleviate some of the headaches between the digital and physical world of photography. The sites provide free editing and cropping tools, as well as albums, picture frames, photo cards and other merchandise. Here are some of these services:

> Ofoto.com
> Shutterfly.com
> dotPhoto.com
> Photopoint.com
> Photos.msn.com

Buy a Digital Picture Frame

A digital picture frame is a traditional frame around a LCD screen (a flat-panel display). The screen is used to display one of several images that you choose. The frames are designed to accommodate new pictures as frequently as you want. The digital picture frames download the images from a server on the Internet. It's a very clever idea. Instead of sending an e-mail message, you can send daily or weekly images or thoughts to people you love in an image format. You can upload the images to a website. Those images can be automatically distributed to any frame within your "network." The concept of ever-changing pictures extends the conventional image and brings the frequency and immediacy closer to loved ones.

A GREAT BABY GIFT

One of the best gifts we received when our daugher was born was a domain name. It came in a little narrow jewelry box, wrapped in tissue paper, and was rolled up and tied with string. On the piece of paper was printed the name of my daughter with a .com extension. It was beautifully presented and ingeniously conceived. Essentially, we were given a destination—a meeting place on the Internet. It had its own address and real estate (disk space) already allocated. The address was personalized to the content that was going to populate it. I immediately saw it as a piece of virtual real estate, and began to fill it with memories. The website has become my online destination and a center for externalizing and distributing our memories.

Had my job just gotten bigger…or better?

Online Destinations

Setting up a destination on the Internet will give you a place to store all the images, text, and media for your online virtual album. From there, you can distribute (share) it in many different ways. Ideally, the perfect destination would be your house, right? Your house has an address and a means to locate it on the map. Your phone number gives easy access to the destination. The phone number you dial routes the calls to your house. Setting up a destination (*domain*) on the web is done much the same way.

On the web, your address is called your *URL* (*Uniform Resource Locator*). The first step towards getting a URL is to decide what its name will be and who is going to set up this service for you. There are a number of resources on the web to do this (**www.register.com**, **www.yahoo.domains.com**, and so on). Each has their own services and products that are designed to make it quick and easy. It's not entirely important that you know what is happening technically, but you should understand the three main steps:

1. Reserve a domain name.
2. Choose your hosting provider.
3. Obtain your FTP instructions.

Now, take a closer look at what you're paying for at each step, and what you get for that payment.

Reserve a Domain Name

Reserving a domain name is the fun part. This becomes the name of the destination and will ultimately be the Yourchoicehere.com of your community. To reserve a domain name, a prepayment of around $20–$30 per year via credit card is required. If you want to name the destination after your child, chances are pretty good that the domain has not yet been taken. You should come up with a few domain names that you would like, prioritizing them accordingly just in case your first choice is taken. Once you choose a name, you will conduct searches for it on a site that will tell you whether it is available or not. There are *a lot* of places on the web to do this. When you conduct these searches, you will be able to see immediately if your choice is available. Be sure also to check if other extensions such as *.net* or *.org* are taken. It is not as important that your domain name be as catchy or memorable as a business site's URL, but like any name, it will define what is going to be found there.

Once you submit the domain search, the forms are automatically sent to InterNIC, the agency that manages the assignment of domain names. If your name is available, domain registration will take 24–48 hours. You then become the domain owner. To keep the domain name, you will need to pay the annual fee of $20 annually, otherwise, the ownership is relinquished and your rights to the domain name might be lost.

Choose Your Hosting Provider

The next step in setting up a URL destination is to choose how your site will be hosted. This is a critical decision. Again, there are hundreds of companies that provide this service. When you sign up with a web hosting company, you are basically leasing hard disk space on their web server. This disk space is used to store all your website files (images, movies, text, and so on). This becomes the actual location that will hold your files. The things you want to think about here are:

> Cost
> Reliability
> Customer service
> Data backup
> Extra services, such as free e-mail accounts

Most companies that are in the hosting business take this very seriously because they market to businesses that pay top dollar for these services. If you know a friend who has a server, you can ask that person if he or she would host a website for you cheaply. Setting this up might not be as turnkey, but you'll save some money. Expect to pay anywhere from $10–$40 per month for a basic, secure, and reliable hosting plan. Also check with the Internet service provider (ISP) that supplies your Internet access. Often your ISP will give you free disk space to host a website. The only downside is that your ISP will give you a predetermined domain name, and it's usually not very exciting.

Obtain your FTP instructions

When you are set up with a domain name and a hosting provider, you will need a way to access that computer server to copy your content onto that site. Usually, you'll receive an automated e-mail message with instructions when you sign up with one of the hosting companies. The company usually follows up by snail mail and gives you the vital information. Don't be alarmed if the company bills you many months in advance for the hosting.

Obtaining a domain name is worth the investment and the time. To put it into perspective, about two weeks of lattes costs the same as securing one year of online real estate. Use it as an investment, and think of it as property. It will not appreciate monetarily, but the value you will find will be in the community and satisfaction it brings you.

While this sounds like a simple endeavor, it can be quite intimidating if you have not done it before. If you're new to creating a website, go to your local bookstore and get a beginner's book on building websites. Also check the website of your Internet service provider, and read the information available online about creating your own web space.

Blogging is becoming an increasingly contextual and immediate medium. The examples here are taken from a research project developed by the Social Computing Group in Microsoft Research.

Blogging: What is it?

by Sean Kelly, Researcher for the Microsoft Social Computing Group

One popular destination for delivering and sharing your memories online is a *weblog* or online journal. Nicknamed *blogs*, these sites are popular ways for people to post their thoughts and recount moments of their lives that might be of interest to others. Blogs are generally composed of sequences of text and images accompanied by the date of posting online, profile information about the author, and links to other sites the author wishes to promote. Blogs form a chronology of your daily posts in the format of quick HTML posts that appear in the browser within a specialized publishing layout that is usually provided by third-party visual templates. As the blogging phenomenon grows in popularity, many companies have provided additional services such as hosting the text content on customized URLs.

Today, blogs increasingly use digital images and are designed with rich media such as sound or video as a way of projecting the author's personality online. They are used to tell personal stories, and many blogs are becoming more like social networks whose participants share their ideas together and link to each other in communities of thought. Some blogs are private only to the authors' trusted readers, but most are openly visible to an audience ranging from friends and relatives to Internet users at large.

The distinction between blogs and other websites or personal home pages is in the highly recognizable design elements and time-based formatting. The most current material usually appears automatically at the top, and recent ones follow in chronological order.

Blogs fulfill an important role in communicating to people you might not contact directly on a regular basis, and blogs give them a rich context to keep in touch with the author and feel connected to them. A popular pursuit of blog authors is tracking one's audience, seeing who comes regularly, and providing feedback tools where the visitors can add their own comments and responses.

Sometimes the most interesting and relevant content on the blog isn't the posts, but the responses. The audience comes to consume the presence of itself in a feedback loop between the audience and the author. This can give an incredibly rich sense of presence and connection to the people involved, as with photographs and other media. Blogs can provide a much more powerful means of expression than e-mail or instant messaging because they allow conversations and media to be serendipitously discovered and added to the original media by the intended audience.

Blogs are becoming deeply visual experiences, to communicate at a glance everything the author wishes us to see.

VISUAL BLOGGING

Many sites have sprung up to support visual blogging and the ability to host images and present them in a richly designed manner. At the same time, social websites such as friendster or ryze provide ways of reaching out to and showing connections to friends and associates online. These sites host images of people at work and play as well as their communications to each other in a public sphere. The end result of these sites, blogs, and social networks alike is to allow people to stay connected and to make new connections online. Blogs and social network sites are rapidly evolving into personal media streams that use rich media such as digital photos, sound, and communications history to project one's personality online in a very effective manner. Templates for design and layout of personal media abound, as do tools and services to make them available to a wide audience. As the concept of blogging grows richer, the Internet provides an essential means of letting people connect to you in more meaningful ways than ever before.

Sean Kelly is the lead researcher responsible for the development and creation of "MyWallop," a research project designed to allow users to share photos, chat with friends, and create and update visual blogs using dynamic media.

For a list blogging resources, visit:
www.futureofmemories.com

Appendix Checklist

☐ Prepare your plan.

☐ Write a dedication/mission statement.

☐ Set up e-mail/instant messaging.

☐ Set up an online photo account.

☐ Find/locate an online destination.

index

A

acquiring images, 105–106
Adobe Photoshop Album, 162–165
   creating books, 164–165
   keywording, 132
annotating
   context, 136–137
   digital images, 130–133
arranging
   bouquet model, 38
   progressive context model, 39
   spine with ribs model, 38
audience, identifying, 13
audio (slide shows), 174
authenticity (documentary style), 34
authoring while browsing, 21

B

basic storytelling, 36–42
batch rename, 14
black-and-white shooting, 75
Bouquet Model, 38
browse and grab, 14
browsing
   authoring while, 21
   digital images, 126–129

C

camera placement, horizon lines, 84–88
camera settings, 78–82
cell phones, 188
CF (compact flash) card, 166–167
chalk drawings (example), 16–17
changing
   film and settings, 71
   point of view, 73
checklist, storytelling, 54
children, photographing, 101

choosing
   context, 17–21
   images to keep, 145
   in-camera, 61
   locations, 67
   natural selection, 148–149
collages, 160–161
color, 95–96
   near infrared, 96
compact flash. See CF (compact flash) card
composition, 102–104
   elements, 102
consistency while shooting, 77
context
   choosing, 17–21
   color, 19
   objects, 19
   perspective, 19
   time, 19
crafting a scene, 40–41
   clone and assemble, 40
   isolating the pieces, 40
   observation, 40
creating
   dynamic media, 182–183
   effective images, 55–116
cropping images, 112
custom prints and collage, 160–161

D

database models
   storing images, 123, 134
   views, 135
depth of field, 102
digital images
   retrieving, 126–129
   sharing, 151–190
digital picture frames, 186

direction
   lines, 102
   motion, 102
displays, smart, 186
disposable shooting, 63
documentary style, 29–35
   authenticity, 34
   defined, 30
   immediacy, 31
   intimacy, 32
   three principles, 35
duplicate and edit the page, 14
DVD/CD players, 185
dynamic media, creating, 182–183

E

e-mail, effective, 171
edit and optimize, 14
editing
   automation, 109
   collections, 146–147
   images on your computer, 107–115
   selective focus, 111
elements
   of composition, 102
   shared by great photos, 58–59
Europe by themes (example), 43
events
   noticing what goes on around you, 42–53
   organizing, 10

F

family tree (example), 141
film, changing, 71
finding your audience, 13
flash
   effective, 92
   fill, 93

flexibility (documentary style), 35
focal point, 102
focus, selective, 111
folders, organizing digital images, 124–125

G

getting closer (documentary style), 35
getting started (example), 12
great photos, shared elements, 58–59

H

hard copies, sharing, 156–165
horizon lines
    camera placement, 84–88
    land and cityscapes, 84–85
    people and places, 86–87

I

identifying audience, 13
images
    acquiring, 105–106
    creating effective, 55–116
    cropping effectively, 112
    editing on your computer, 107–115
    processing, 114–115
    retrieving, 126–129
    transferring to your computer, 105–106
immediacy (documentary style), 31
immersive experiences (slide shows), 174
index, simple. See spine
interface, timeline, 9
intimacy (documentary style), 32
iZotope PhotonShow, creating dynamic
    media, 182–183

K

keywording
    digital images, 130–133
    using Adobe Photoshop Album, 132
Kilimanjaro (example of storage scheme), 129

L

land and cityscapes, horizon lines, 84–85
libraries
    digital image, 123
    editing, 146–147
life building, 118–122
life events, organizing, 10
life library, organizing, 117–150
lifeboating, 145
light, 89–95
    effective flash, 92
    fill flash, 93
    lighting situations, 90
location and mapping, 138–143
location and travels (example of storage
    scheme), 129
locations
    choosing, 67
    solving problems, 69

M

Macromedia Flash. See iZotope PhotonShow,
    creating dynamic media
mapping. See also location and mapping
    defined, 140
    examples, 141–143
media facets, 135. See also movies and
    media
metadata, 130
Microsoft Digital Image Suite 9, 160–161
Microsoft Plus! Photo Story. See Plus!
    Photo Story
mobile phones, 188

N

narrative structures. See planning, structure
near-infrared photography, 96
new film, the, 166–167

O

organizing
    date vs. topic, 124–125
    images on your computer, 122–125
    life events, 10
    life library, 117–150
    by location, 138–143
    using folders, 124–125

P

patterns, using in storytelling, 149
people and places, horizon lines, 86–87
personal video recorders (PVRs), 185
photo editing, 146–147
photo receivers, 186–187
photographing children, 101
planning
    big picture, 36–37
    story stick figures, 36–42
    structure, 36–37
Plus! Photo Story, 22–23, 171
point of view, changing, 73
Portable Media Center, 188–189

models
    Bouquet, 38
    database, 123
    Progressive Context, 39
    Spine with Ribs, 38
movies and media, 178–179
moving around (documentary style), 35
Multimedia Messaging (MMS), 188
My First Real Story (example), 24–25
MyPublisher, creating books, 164–165

presentations. *See slide shows*
prints
    conventional, 156
    custom, 160–161
    home printers, 158–165
    professional, 156
processing images, 114–115
Progressive Context Model, 39
project, beginning, 26–27
publish (post the files), 14

R

retrieving digital images, 126–129

S

San Francisco vacation (example), 142
scale and contrast, 97–99
scenes, crafting, 40–41
sequences, shooting, 65
sequential stills (slide shows), 174
settings
    camera, 78–82
    changing, 71
share map, 154–155
sharing
    Adobe Photoshop Album, 162–165
    digital images, 151–190
    formats, 154
    hard copies, 156–165
    iZotope PhotonShow, 182–183
    Microsoft Picture It! Digital Image Suite 9, 160–161
    mobile memories, 188–189
    Multimedia Messaging (MMS), 188
    over time, 168–169
    soft copies, 170–189

shooting
    black and white, 75
    disposable, 63
    sequence, 65
simple index. *See spine*
situations, lighting, 90
slide shows, 172–184
    audio, 174
    immersive experiences, 174
    sequential stills, 174
    templates, 180–184
    transitions, 174
    typography, 174
    viewing full screen, 174
smart displays, 186
soft copies, sharing, 170–189
spine, 14
Spine with Ribs Model, 38
starting (example), 12
stick figures (storytelling), 36–42
storytelling, 1–54
    checklist, 54
    stick figures, 36–42
    using patterns, 149
style, documentary, 29–35

T

techniques
    batch rename, 14
    browse and grab, 14
    duplicate and edit the page, 14
    edit and optimize, 14
    publish (post the files), 14
    update the text, 14
    for working quickly, 14, 83
templates (slide shows), 180–184

themes
    blur, 46
    chocolate croissant, 44
    expressively unique, 52
    food and beverages, 49
    local motion, 45
    Louvre, the, 48
    maps, plane tickets, and lists, 51
    memories, 53
    table settings, 47
    water, 50
timeline interface, 9
transferring images to your computer, 105–106
transitions (slide shows), 174
traveling
    Europe by themes, 43
    themes, 42–53
typography (slide shows), 174

V

values, 102
views
    full screen, 174
    thumbnails, 121

W

working quickly, 14, 83

Learn how to get the job done every day—
faster, smarter, and easier!

**Faster Smarter
Digital Photography**
ISBN: 0-7356-1872-0
U.S.A. $19.99
Canada $28.99

**Faster Smarter
Microsoft® Office XP**
ISBN: 0-7356-1862-3
U.S.A. $19.99
Canada $28.99

**Faster Smarter
Microsoft Windows® XP**
ISBN: 0-7356-1857-7
U.S.A. $19.99
Canada $28.99

**Faster Smarter
Home Networking**
ISBN: 0-7356-1869-0
U.S.A. $19.99
Canada $28.99

Discover how to do exactly what you do with computers and technology—faster, smarter, and easier—with FASTER SMARTER books from Microsoft Press! They're your everyday guides for learning the practicalities of how to make technology work the way you want—fast. Their language is friendly and down-to-earth, with no jargon or silly chatter, and with accurate how-to information that's easy to absorb and apply. Use the concise explanations, easy numbered steps, and visual examples to understand exactly what you need to do to get the job done—whether you're using a PC at home or in business, capturing and sharing digital still images, getting a home network running, or finishing other tasks.

**Microsoft Press has other FASTER SMARTER titles to help you get the job done every day.
To learn more about the full line of Microsoft Press® products, please visit us at:**

microsoft.com/mspress

Work smarter—conquer your software *from the inside out!*

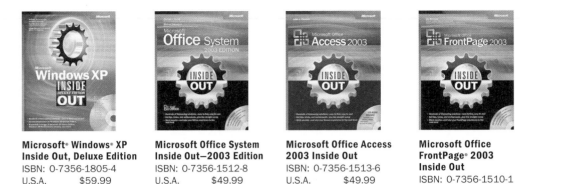

Microsoft® Windows® XP Inside Out, Deluxe Edition
ISBN: 0-7356-1805-4
U.S.A. $59.99
Canada $86.99

Microsoft Office System Inside Out—2003 Edition
ISBN: 0-7356-1512-8
U.S.A. $49.99
Canada $72.99

Microsoft Office Access 2003 Inside Out
ISBN: 0-7356-1513-6
U.S.A. $49.99
Canada $72.99

Microsoft Office FrontPage® 2003 Inside Out
ISBN: 0-7356-1510-1
U.S.A. $49.99
Canada $72.99

Hey, you know your way around a desktop. Now dig into the new Microsoft Office products and the Windows XP operating system and *really* put your PC to work! These supremely organized software reference titles pack hundreds of timesaving solutions, troubleshooting tips and tricks, and handy workarounds into a concise, fast-answer format. They're all muscle and no fluff. All this comprehensive information goes deep into the nooks and crannies of each Office application and Windows XP feature. And every INSIDE OUT title includes a CD-ROM packed with bonus content such as tools and utilities, demo programs, sample scripts, batch programs, an eBook containing the book's complete text, and more! Discover the best and fastest ways to perform everyday tasks, and challenge yourself to new levels of software mastery!

Microsoft Press has other INSIDE OUT titles to help you get the job done every day:

Microsoft Office Excel 2003 Programming Inside Out
ISBN: 0-7356-1985-9

Microsoft Office Word 2003 Inside Out
ISBN: 0-7356-1515-2

Microsoft Office Excel 2003 Inside Out
ISBN: 0-7356-1511-X

Microsoft Office Outlook 2003® Inside Out
ISBN: 0-7356-1514-4

Microsoft Office Project 2003 Inside Out
ISBN: 0-7356-1958-1

Microsoft Office Visio® 2003 Inside Out
ISBN: 0-7356-1516-0

Microsoft Windows XP Networking Inside Out
ISBN: 0-7356-1652-3

Microsoft Windows Security Inside Out for Windows XP and Windows 2000
ISBN: 0-7356-1632-9

To learn more about the full line of Microsoft Press® products, please visit us at:

microsoft.com/mspress/

Your *fast-answers, no jargon* guides to Windows XP and Office XP

Get the fast facts that make learning the Microsoft® Windows® XP operating system and Microsoft Office XP applications plain and simple! Numbered steps show exactly what to do, and color screen shots keep you on track. *Handy Tips* teach easy techniques and shortcuts, while quick *Try This!* exercises put your learning to work. And *Caution* notes help keep you out of trouble, so you won't get bogged down. No matter what you need to do, you'll find the simplest ways to get it done with PLAIN & SIMPLE!

Microsoft Windows® XP Plain & Simple
ISBN 0-7356-1525-X

Microsoft Office XP Plain & Simple
ISBN 0-7356-1449-0

Microsoft Word Version 2002 Plain & Simple
ISBN 0-7356-1450-4

Microsoft Excel Version 2002 Plain & Simple
ISBN 0-7356-1451-2

Microsoft Outlook® Version 2002 Plain & Simple
ISBN 0-7356-1452-0

Microsoft FrontPage® Version 2002 Plain & Simple
ISBN 0-7356-1453-9

Microsoft Access Version 2002 Plain & Simple
ISBN 0-7356-1454-7

U.S.A.	$19.99
Canada	$28.99

Microsoft®

microsoft.com/mspress

Get a **Free**
e-mail newsletter, updates,
special offers, links to related books,
and more when you
register online!

Register your Microsoft Press® title on our Web site and you'll get a FREE subscription to our e-mail newsletter, *Microsoft Press Book Connections.* You'll find out about newly released and upcoming books and learning tools, online events, software downloads, special offers and coupons for Microsoft Press customers, and information about major Microsoft® product releases. You can also read useful additional information about all the titles we publish, such as detailed book descriptions, tables of contents and indexes, sample chapters, links to related books and book series, author biographies, and reviews by other customers.

Registration is easy. Just visit this Web page and fill in your information:

http://www.microsoft.com/mspress/register

Microsoft®

- -